DREAMS INTERPRETATION GUIDE

A Comprehensive Guide to Dream Interpretation
Zodiac Odyssey, Published
By Daniel Sanjurjo, 2023.

While every precaution has been taken in the preparation of this book, the publisher assumes no responsibility for errors or omissions, or for damages resulting from the use of the information contained herein.

DREAMS INTERPRETATION GUIDE

First edition. November 22, 2023.

Written by Daniel Sanjurjo.

Table of Contents

Introduction:

Unlocking the Enigma of Dreams

Welcome to a journey into the enigmatic realm of dreams, where the boundaries between reality and the subconscious blur, and the mind unveils its most profound mysteries. In this exploration, we embark on a quest to decipher the age-old language of dreams, seeking to understand their significance and unravel the stories woven in the fabric of our minds.

This comprehensive guide to dream interpretation is a culmination of knowledge, research, and the shared experiences of dreamers throughout history. Our goal is simple: to provide you with a window into the complex world of dreams, delving into their meanings, symbolism, and the profound impact they have on our lives.

As you turn the pages of this book, you will encounter a rich tapestry of insights, from the historical significance of dreams to the cultural variations in their interpretation. We delve into the multifaceted nature of dreams, exploring their cognitive, emotional, and therapeutic aspects, and the intricate role they play in our psyche.

While we journey through the chapters, we'll also peek into the modern world, where technology, psychology, and cultural shifts have left their indelible mark on the way we perceive and analyze dreams. Emerging technologies, interdisciplinary approaches, and the evolving landscape of psychology offer us a glimpse into the potential future of dream exploration.

The dream state is a place of wonder where personal growth, self-exploration, and creativity converge. It continues to be a source of fascination, a canvas for artists and writers, and a tool for gaining self-awareness and understanding.

Join us as we unlock the enigma of dreams, for they are not mere figments of the night but gateways to our inner world. The stories they tell, the emotions they stir, and the insights they offer are a testament to the infinite depths of the human mind.

In this book, we invite you to explore the timeless, the contemporary, and the boundless future of dream exploration. Whether you're a seasoned dreamer or a curious novice, this book promises a journey that will expand your understanding of the mysterious world that unfolds when we close our eyes and surrender to the night.

Are you ready to begin this fascinating exploration? Let's open the door to the realm of dreams and step into a world where the subconscious reigns supreme.

IN THE ENIGMATIC REALM of human consciousness, dreams stand as cryptic narratives, woven by the intricate tapestry of the mind. An exploration into the labyrinth of these nocturnal tales reveals the profound "Meaning of Dreams." It is in these fleeting moments, where the surreal intermingles with the subconscious, that we seek to decipher the enigma that is dream interpretation.

To comprehend the "Meaning of Dreams," one must embark on a journey that transcends time and culture. This chapter embarks on a quest through the historical annals of dream analysis, unearthing the diverse perspectives that have illuminated the path to understanding the ethereal.

As the ancients pondered the symbols and visions that danced in the night, we will delve into the dreams of Sumerians, Egyptians, and Greeks, finding threads of commonality and distinction. The sands of time may have shifted, but the curiosity of humankind remains unaltered.

Furthermore, we explore the notion that dream interpretation is not confined by geographic boundaries. Different cultures and societies have painted their unique brushstrokes on the canvas of dream meanings. From the mysticism of the East to the scientific rigidity of the West, dream interpretation has taken various forms.

In this chapter, we lay the foundation for understanding dreams. We consider the "Meaning of Dreams" not merely as a singular definition but as a multifaceted prism, reflecting the many facets of human existence. Whether you seek answers in ancient scrolls, modern psychology, or personal introspection, the enigma of dreams remains an intricate tapestry, waiting to be unraveled.

Sigmund Freud's Pioneering Insights

Sigmund Freud, the renowned Austrian neurologist and father of psychoanalysis, made profound contributions to the field of dream analysis. His work on the interpretation of dreams, published in his seminal book "The Interpretation of Dreams" in 1899, marked a pivotal moment in the history of understanding the human psyche.

Freud proposed that dreams were the "royal road to the unconscious," and his theories opened up new avenues for exploring the inner workings of the human mind. He believed that dreams were the result of unconscious desires and wishes, often hidden from our waking consciousness.

One of Freud's key concepts was the division of the mind into the conscious, the preconscious, and the unconscious. He argued that dreams were a direct pathway to the unconscious, allowing individuals to explore and confront suppressed thoughts, memories, and emotions.

In his book, Freud introduced the idea of dream symbolism, suggesting that many elements in dreams had hidden meanings. He believed that symbols in dreams could represent repressed desires and conflicts, and that the analysis of these symbols could lead to a better understanding of the dreamer's inner world.

Furthermore, Freud's work on dream interpretation laid the groundwork for the development of psychoanalysis, a field that continues to influence psychology and psychiatry to this day. His pioneering insights into the significance of dreams have left an enduring mark on our understanding of the human psyche.

While Freud's theories have been the subject of debate and revision over the years, his work remains a cornerstone in the study of dreams and the exploration of the unconscious mind

Chapter 1: The Meaning of Dreams

Key Points:
Dreams are intricate narratives that reveal the workings of the subconscious mind.

The exploration of dream interpretation spans various cultures and historical periods.

Understanding the meaning of dreams requires a multifaceted approach, taking into account different perspectives.

Highlighted Important Sections:

The Enigmatic Realm of Dreams

In the enigmatic realm of human consciousness, dreams stand as cryptic narratives, woven by the intricate tapestry of the mind. An exploration into the labyrinth of these nocturnal tales reveals the profound "Meaning of Dreams."

A Journey Through Time and Culture

To comprehend the "Meaning of Dreams," one must embark on a journey that transcends time and culture. This chapter delves into the historical annals of dream analysis, unearthing the diverse perspectives that have illuminated the path to understanding the ethereal.

Cultural Perspectives

We explore the notion that dream interpretation is not confined by geographic boundaries. Different cultures and societies have painted their unique brushstrokes on the canvas of dream meanings. From the mysticism of the East to the scientific rigidity of the West, dream interpretation has taken various forms.

The Multifaceted Nature of Dream Interpretation

In this chapter, we lay the foundation for understanding dreams. We consider the "Meaning of Dreams" not merely as a singular definition but as a multifaceted prism, reflecting the many facets of human existence. Whether you seek answers in ancient scrolls, modern psychology, or personal introspection, the enigma of dreams remains an intricate tapestry, waiting to be unraveled.

The Dreamscape Unveiled

Within the fabric of our nightly visions lies a universe of symbolism and emotion, waiting to be deciphered. Dreams are the mirror to our innermost thoughts, fears, and desires. To grasp the "Meaning of Dreams," one must navigate the intricate landscapes of the dreamscape.

Key Points:

• Dreams reflect our inner thoughts, emotions, and subconscious.

• The dreamscape is a complex terrain filled with symbolism and significance.

• Understanding the dreamscape is essential for meaningful dream interpretation.

Highlighted Important Sections:

Unveiling the Subconscious Dreams are the mirror to our innermost thoughts, fears, and desires. They offer a glimpse into the hidden recesses of our minds, often revealing thoughts and emotions we may not consciously acknowledge.

Symbolism and Significance The dreamscape is not a straightforward narrative but a realm of symbolism and significance. Objects, people, and places in dreams often hold hidden meanings, waiting to be unraveled by those who seek to understand.

The Challenge of Interpretation Interpreting dreams is not a simple task. It requires a deep understanding of the dreamscape, the ability to recognize symbols, and an appreciation for the complexities of human psychology. Dream interpretation is both an art and a science, requiring patience and insight.

As we move forward in this exploration of dream interpretation, we will delve deeper into the mechanisms that govern the dreamscape and how these can be unraveled to reveal the "Meaning of Dreams."

DECIPHERING THE DREAM Symbols

In the enigmatic world of dreams, symbols reign supreme. As we journey through the "Meaning of Dreams," it becomes apparent that symbols are the very essence of the dreamscape. Deciphering these symbols is a fundamental step in unlocking the hidden messages within our dreams.

Key Points:

• Symbols play a central role in the world of dreams.

• Understanding dream symbols is crucial for dream interpretation.

• Different symbols can hold diverse meanings for individuals.

Highlighted Important Sections:

The Language of Dreams In the realm of dreams, symbolism is the primary language. Objects, animals, people, and even actions in dreams often carry deeper meanings. To interpret dreams, one must become fluent in this unique language.

Personal Symbolism While there are common dream symbols with shared meanings, personal symbolism is equally significant. A dream symbol that holds a specific meaning for one person may have a different interpretation for another. This personal aspect of dream interpretation adds depth and complexity to the process.

Universal Symbols Certain symbols have universal significance across cultures and times. Exploring these universal symbols and their meanings offers insights into the shared aspects of the human psyche. Understanding both personal and universal symbolism is essential for comprehensive dream analysis.

The Art of Decoding Deciphering dream symbols is akin to solving puzzles. It requires careful observation, introspection, and an appreciation for the nuances of the human mind. The journey to understanding the "Meaning of Dreams" involves becoming a skilled interpreter of this intricate and symbolic language.

As we venture further into the world of dream interpretation, the importance of symbols and their role in unraveling the enigma of dreams becomes increasingly clear.

The Depths of the Subconscious Mind

To comprehend the "Meaning of Dreams" fully, one must voyage into the depths of the subconscious mind. Here, in the hidden recesses of our thoughts and emotions, lies the source of our dreams. Exploring the subconscious mind is akin to unraveling the mystery at the heart of dream interpretation.

Key Points:

• Dreams originate from the subconscious mind.

• Understanding the subconscious is crucial for interpreting dreams.

• The subconscious is a complex realm of memories, emotions, and desires.

Highlighted Important Sections:

The Birthplace of Dreams Dreams are not random occurrences; they are born from the subconscious. The subconscious mind stores a treasure trove of memories, emotions, and desires, which surface as dreams during the sleeping state.

Emotions in Dreams Emotions often play a central role in dreams. Understanding the emotional landscape of the subconscious is essential for interpreting the underlying messages of dreams. Whether it's fear, joy, or anxiety, emotions in dreams reveal the innermost feelings of the dreamer.

The Influence of Memories Memories, both recent and long-buried, can resurface in dreams. Exploring the connection between memories and dream content provides valuable insights into the "Meaning of Dreams."

The Subconscious Dialogue Interpreting dreams is, in essence, deciphering a dialogue with the subconscious mind. It involves listening to the whispers and shouts of the subconscious, understanding its language, and recognizing the patterns that emerge in dreams.

As we delve deeper into the workings of the subconscious mind, we gain a better understanding of the intricacies that shape our dreams and their significance.

Interpreting the Dreamer's Perspective

In the pursuit of the "Meaning of Dreams," it is essential to appreciate that dream interpretation is not a one-size-fits-all endeavor. The perspective of the dreamer plays a significant role in understanding the messages conveyed by dreams. Each dreamer brings their unique experiences and emotions to the dream analysis process.

Key Points:

• Dream interpretation is a personalized experience.

• The dreamer's perspective and life experiences influence dream meanings.

• A holistic approach to dream analysis considers both the dream's content and the dreamer's individuality.

Highlighted Important Sections:

The Dreamer's Lens Every dreamer views the world through their own unique lens. This lens is formed by personal experiences, beliefs, and emotions. It colors the way dreams are perceived and interpreted. Understanding the dreamer's perspective is crucial in decoding dream messages.

Life Experiences and Dreams Life experiences, both positive and negative, leave imprints on the subconscious mind. These imprints are often mirrored in dreams, reflecting the dreamer's past, present, and future. By recognizing the connections between life experiences and dream content, a deeper understanding of the "Meaning of Dreams" can be reached.

A Holistic Approach Successful dream interpretation requires a holistic approach. It involves examining both the content of the dream and the dreamer's individuality. By weaving these two elements together, a more accurate and insightful interpretation can be achieved.

Empathy and Insight Dream interpreters must possess empathy and insight to comprehend the dreamer's perspective fully. This requires a deep appreciation for the complexities of the human psyche and a willingness to explore the intricacies of each dreamer's unique journey.

As we continue our journey through the world of dream interpretation, we emphasize the importance of understanding the dreamer's perspective and the role it plays in unveiling the "Meaning of Dreams."

The Art of Dream Interpretation

Dream interpretation is not a mere science; it is an art that combines analytical skills with creativity. It is a delicate dance between the rational mind and the imaginative spirit. In this section, we delve into the intricacies of the art of dream interpretation.

Key Points:

• Dream interpretation is both a science and an art.

• Analytical skills and creativity are essential for effective dream analysis.

• Interpretation often involves exploring multiple layers of meaning within a dream.

Highlighted Important Sections:

The Balance of Science and Art Effective dream interpretation requires a harmonious balance between scientific analysis and creative insight. It's the synergy of these two elements that unlocks the "Meaning of Dreams."

Navigating the Layers of Meaning Dreams are not one-dimensional; they often contain multiple layers of meaning. A skilled dream interpreter navigates through these layers, unveiling the intricate messages concealed within the dream's fabric.

The Role of Intuition Intuition is a vital component of dream interpretation. It allows interpreters to tap into their inner wisdom and connect with the dream's deeper significance. Balancing analytical thinking with intuition is key to successful dream analysis.

The Unveiling of Insights Dream interpretation is a journey of self-discovery. As dreamers and interpreters peel away the layers of symbolism, emotions, and memories, they reveal profound insights into the self and the world.

In the realm of dream interpretation, the art lies in the ability to bridge the conscious and the unconscious, the logical and the creative, to unravel the "Meaning of Dreams."

Navigating the Dreamer's Journey

The journey of dream interpretation is akin to navigating uncharted waters. It involves careful exploration, introspection, and a deep connection with the dreamer's experiences and emotions. In this section, we embark on a voyage through the dreamer's journey, shedding light on the complexities of dream analysis.

Key Points:

• Dream interpretation is a journey of exploration and self-discovery.

• The dreamer's journey is deeply personal, marked by emotions, memories, and symbolism.

• Interpreters guide dreamers in unraveling the mysteries of their dreams.

Highlighted Important Sections:

Exploring the Dreamer's Narrative Every dreamer carries a unique narrative within their dreams. This narrative is woven with personal experiences, emotions, and desires. Interpreters play the role of navigators, guiding dreamers through the labyrinth of their own stories.

Emotions as Signposts Emotions are powerful signposts in the dreamer's journey. They highlight the dreamer's state of mind, concerns, and aspirations. Interpreters must skillfully read these emotional cues to understand the dream's deeper meanings.

The Collaborative Effort Dream interpretation is often a collaborative effort between the dreamer and the interpreter. It involves open dialogue, trust, and a shared commitment to exploring the depths of the dreamer's journey.

The Unveiling of Insights As interpreters and dreamers work together to decipher dreams, profound insights are unveiled. These insights offer a clearer perspective on the dreamer's life, challenges, and opportunities for growth.

The journey of dream interpretation is not merely about decoding symbols; it is about connecting with the dreamer's inner world and assisting them in their quest to understand the "Meaning of Dreams."

Interpreting Dreams: A Guided Process

Effective dream interpretation is a guided process that involves a series of steps, each designed to unveil the layers of meaning within a dream. In this section, we outline the steps and strategies that form the framework for interpreting dreams.

Key Points:

• Dream interpretation follows a structured process.

• Steps in dream interpretation include recalling the dream, identifying symbols, and exploring emotions.

• The process encourages a comprehensive understanding of the dream's significance.

Highlighted Important Sections:

Recalling the Dream The first step in dream interpretation is to recall the dream as vividly as possible. This involves noting details, events, and emotions that occurred within the dream.

Identifying Symbols Dreams are rich in symbolism. The dream interpreter must identify and analyze the symbols present in the dream, understanding their personal and universal significance.

Exploring Emotions Emotions provide valuable clues in dream interpretation. Analyzing the emotions experienced during the dream sheds light on the dreamer's inner state.

Seeking Patterns and Connections, Interpreters look for patterns and connections within the dream, such as recurring themes or symbols. These patterns offer insights into the dream's deeper meanings.

Considering Personal Experiences and memories are often intertwined with dream content. Examining the dreamer's life and experiences can provide additional context for interpretation.

Reflecting on the Dream's Role Dream interpretation goes beyond deciphering symbols; it involves reflecting on the dream's role in the dreamer's life, addressing personal challenges, and fostering personal growth.

Dream interpretation is a structured and thoughtful process that empowers dreamers to explore the "Meaning of Dreams" with guidance and insight.

Case Studies: Understanding Dream Interpretation in Action

To gain a deeper understanding of the art of dream interpretation, we turn our attention to real-life case studies. These examples offer practical insights into how the process of dream interpretation is applied, showcasing its effectiveness in unraveling the "Meaning of Dreams."

Key Points:

• Real-life case studies provide practical examples of dream interpretation.

• Each case study highlights the unique challenges and insights offered by dream interpretation.

• The process of interpretation is brought to life through these tangible examples.

Highlighted Important Sections:

Case Study 1: The Recurring Nightmare In this case study, we delve into a recurring nightmare experienced by a dreamer. We explore the dream's content, its emotional impact, and how interpretation revealed hidden fears and unresolved issues.

Case Study 2: The Dream of Flying This case study centers around a dream where the dreamer finds themselves flying freely in the sky. We examine the dream's symbolism, emotions, and the personal significance of this extraordinary experience.

Case Study 3: The Enigmatic Symbol In the third case study, we tackle a dream containing a puzzling symbol. We follow the journey of deciphering the symbol's meaning, demonstrating how dream interpretation can unveil the hidden messages within the dream.

The Power of Interpretation Through these real-life case studies, we witness the transformative power of dream interpretation. It is a tool for self-discovery, personal growth, and finding solutions to life's challenges. These case studies exemplify how dream interpretation brings the "Meaning of Dreams" to life.

Dream Interpretation Resources: Navigating the World of Dreams

Dream interpretation is a vast field, and dreamers often seek guidance and resources to assist them on their journey to understand the "Meaning of Dreams." In this section, we explore the various tools, references, and professionals available to aid in dream interpretation.

Key Points:

• Dream interpretation resources provide valuable support for dreamers.

• These resources include books, websites, and professionals.

• Choosing the right resources can enhance the dream interpretation process.

Highlighted Important Sections:

Dream Interpretation Books We discuss the significance of dream interpretation books as valuable references for both beginners and experienced interpreters. A list of recommended books is provided, offering dreamers a starting point for their exploration.

Online Dream Interpretation Websites In the digital age, the internet offers a plethora of dream interpretation websites. We highlight the importance of reliable online resources and recommend specific websites for dreamers to explore.

Professional Dream Interpreters For those seeking personalized guidance, professional dream interpreters offer valuable insights. We explore the role of dream therapists, psychologists, and counselors in aiding dreamers on their journey.

Community and Support Groups Dream interpretation often benefits from sharing experiences and insights with others. We introduce the concept of dream interpretation communities and support groups, which provide a platform for collaboration and learning.

Choosing the Right Resources Selecting the right dream interpretation resources is crucial. We offer guidance on how dreamers can assess the reliability and suitability of resources to enhance their dream interpretation journey.

Navigating the world of dreams is enriched by accessing the right resources, and this section provides dreamers with a roadmap to do so.

Chapter 2: Types of Dreams

Dreams are diverse and multifaceted, reflecting the complexities of the human mind. In this chapter, we explore the various types of dreams that populate the nocturnal landscape. By understanding these different dream experiences, we gain insights into the rich tapestry of the human subconscious.

Key Points:

• Different types of dreams provide distinct experiences and insights.

• Common dream categories include lucid dreams, nightmares, and recurring dreams.

• Each dream type has unique characteristics and can offer valuable information about the dreamer's inner world.

Highlighted Important Sections:

Lucid Dreams: A World of Awareness Lucid dreams are a unique category where the dreamer becomes aware of their dream state. We delve into the characteristics of lucid dreams and the potential for self-discovery and control within this fascinating dream realm.

Nightmares: Confronting Fears and Anxieties Nightmares, characterized by vivid and distressing content, often provoke intense emotions. We explore the nature of nightmares and how they serve as a window into our deepest fears and anxieties.

Recurring Dreams: Messages from the Subconscious Recurring dreams are dreams that revisit the dreamer time and again. We examine the significance of recurring dreams and how they hold recurring messages from the subconscious.

Other Dream Categories Beyond the well-known dream types, there exist numerous other dream categories, each with its own unique qualities. We briefly touch upon some of these categories, such as epic dreams, prophetic dreams, and more.

This chapter sheds light on the various types of dreams, helping dreamers and interpreters comprehend the diverse experiences and messages that arise within the realm of the subconscious.

Epic Dreams: The Journey of the Soul

Epic dreams are a category of dreams that transcend the ordinary and venture into extraordinary realms. In this section, we explore the unique characteristics and significance of epic dreams, offering a deeper understanding of their role in the world of dream interpretation.

Key Points:

• Epic dreams are characterized by their extraordinary nature and often feel like grand adventures.

• These dreams may involve mythological themes, archetypal figures, and a sense of profundity.

• Epic dreams have the potential to provide profound insights and personal transformation.

Highlighted Important Sections:

The Mythical Landscape of Epic Dreams Epic dreams often transport dreamers to a mythical landscape where gods, heroes, and archetypal figures come to life. We explore the symbolism and cultural significance of these dream elements.

The Sense of Profundity Epic dreams are marked by their profound impact on the dreamer. We delve into how these dreams can evoke strong emotions, a sense of awe, and a feeling of deep significance.

Interpreting Epic Dreams Dream interpretation for epic dreams involves navigating a unique terrain. We discuss the strategies and considerations for interpreting these extraordinary dream experiences, emphasizing their potential for personal transformation.

As we explore epic dreams, we uncover their remarkable qualities and the ways in which they can shape the dreamer's understanding of the "Meaning of Dreams."

Prophetic Dreams: Glimpses of the Future

Prophetic dreams have long held a mystique, as they appear to offer glimpses into events yet to come. In this section, we delve into the world of prophetic dreams, exploring their characteristics, potential interpretations, and the intriguing question of whether they truly reveal the future.

Key Points:

• Prophetic dreams are dreams that seem to foretell future events or outcomes.

• The interpretation of prophetic dreams often involves a balance between skepticism and belief.

• Various cultures and historical accounts include examples of prophetic dreams.

Highlighted Important Sections:

The Nature of Prophetic Dreams We examine the distinctive features of prophetic dreams, such as their vividness, the sense of déjà vu, and the emotional impact they can have on the dreamer.

Interpreting Prophetic Dreams Interpreting prophetic dreams can be a complex process, as it involves considering the potential symbolic meanings and discerning whether the dream genuinely foretells the future. We explore the strategies and perspectives used in interpreting these enigmatic dreams.

Historical and Cultural Significance Throughout history, prophetic dreams have played a significant role in shaping beliefs and decisions. We highlight examples from various cultures and historical accounts where prophetic dreams held great importance.

The Mystery of Prophetic Dreams While the mystery of prophetic dreams remains, this section aims to provide a balanced understanding of their nature, significance, and the questions they raise about the boundaries of dream interpretation.

Healing Dreams: Restoration of Mind and Body

Healing dreams are a distinct category of dreams that hold the potential to bring solace, comfort, and even physical or emotional healing to the dreamer. In this section, we explore the unique characteristics and therapeutic aspects of healing dreams.

Key Points:

• Healing dreams are dreams that provide solace, comfort, or contribute to physical and emotional healing.

• These dreams often contain themes of recovery, support, or the resolution of inner conflicts.

• Healing dreams can offer a sense of renewal and well-being to the dreamer.

Highlighted Important Sections:

The Nature of Healing Dreams We delve into the defining characteristics of healing dreams, such as their focus on recovery, comfort, and the resolution of emotional or physical challenges.

Emotional Healing Through Dreams Many healing dreams are focused on emotional healing, providing a space for the dreamer to work through unresolved feelings, traumas, or inner conflicts. We explore how these dreams contribute to the dreamer's emotional well-being.

Physical Healing and Dreams Some healing dreams are associated with physical recovery or the alleviation of physical ailments. We discuss the potential relationship between dream content and the healing process.

Interpreting Healing Dreams Interpreting healing dreams involves recognizing their therapeutic qualities and understanding the role they play in the dreamer's overall well-being. We discuss strategies for interpreting these restorative dream experiences.

As we explore healing dreams, we gain insights into their comforting and rejuvenating nature, highlighting the role they play in the broader spectrum of dream experiences.

Evolving Dreams: A Journey of Transformation

Evolving dreams are a category of dreams that revolve around personal growth and transformation. In this section, we explore the unique characteristics and significance of evolving dreams, emphasizing their role in the dreamer's journey towards self-improvement.

Key Points:

• Evolving dreams are dreams that focus on personal growth and transformation.

• These dreams often contain themes of change, development, and self-discovery.

• Evolving dreams can inspire the dreamer to make positive life changes.

Highlighted Important Sections:

The Nature of Evolving Dreams We delve into the defining characteristics of evolving dreams, such as their emphasis on change, self-improvement, and the exploration of new possibilities.

Self-Discovery Through Dreams Evolving dreams often serve as a pathway to self-discovery. They encourage the dreamer to explore their inner potential, aspirations, and the pursuit of personal goals.

Positive Life Changes Evolving dreams can be a catalyst for positive life changes. We explore how these dreams inspire the dreamer to take action, make decisions, and embrace opportunities for transformation.

Interpreting Evolving Dreams Interpreting evolving dreams involves recognizing their potential for personal growth and understanding the role they play in the dreamer's journey towards self-improvement. We discuss strategies for interpreting these transformative dream experiences.

As we explore evolving dreams, we uncover their power to inspire change, personal growth, and the pursuit of a more fulfilling life.

Visitation Dreams: Encounters with the Departed

Visitation dreams are a remarkable category of dreams where dreamers believe they have encountered loved ones who have passed away. In this section, we explore the unique characteristics and emotional significance of visitation dreams.

Key Points:

• Visitation dreams are dreams where dreamers feel they have had contact with deceased loved ones.

• These dreams often provide comfort, closure, and the sense of connection with the departed.

• The emotional and spiritual aspects of visitation dreams are explored.

Highlighted Important Sections:

The Nature of Visitation Dreams We delve into the defining characteristics of visitation dreams, such as the vividness of the encounters, the emotions they evoke, and the belief in a spiritual connection with the departed.

Emotional Healing and Closure Visitation dreams can offer emotional healing and a sense of closure to those who have lost loved ones. We discuss how these dreams contribute to the dreamer's emotional well-being.

Beliefs and Spirituality Visitation dreams often intersect with beliefs about the afterlife and spirituality. We explore the diverse cultural and spiritual perspectives on visitation dreams.

Interpreting Visitation Dreams Interpreting visitation dreams involves understanding their emotional significance and recognizing their potential for bringing solace and connection to the dreamer. We discuss strategies for interpreting these deeply emotional dream experiences.

As we explore visitation dreams, we gain insights into their potential for providing comfort and spiritual connection to those who have experienced loss.

Epic Dreams: The Journey of the Soul

Epic dreams are a category of dreams that transcend the ordinary and venture into extraordinary realms. In this section, we explore the unique characteristics and significance of epic dreams, offering a deeper understanding of their role in the world of dream interpretation.

Key Points:

• Epic dreams are characterized by their extraordinary nature and often feel like grand adventures.

• These dreams may involve mythological themes, archetypal figures, and a sense of profundity.

• Epic dreams have the potential to provide profound insights and personal transformation.

Highlighted Important Sections:

The Mythical Landscape of Epic Dreams Epic dreams often transport dreamers to a mythical landscape where gods, heroes, and archetypal figures come to life. We explore the symbolism and cultural significance of these dream elements.

The Sense of Profundity Epic dreams are marked by their profound impact on the dreamer. We delve into how these dreams can evoke strong emotions, a sense of awe, and a feeling of deep significance.

Interpreting Epic Dreams Dream interpretation for epic dreams involves navigating a unique terrain. We discuss the strategies and considerations for interpreting these extraordinary dream experiences, emphasizing their potential for personal transformation.

As we explore epic dreams, we uncover their remarkable qualities and the ways in which they can shape the dreamer's understanding of the "Meaning of Dreams."

The Mystery of Dream Categories

In this section, we explore the intricacies and mysteries surrounding dream categories. While we have discussed several distinct types of dreams, we also recognize that dream experiences are highly personal and can often transcend clear categorization. This section delves into the blurred boundaries of dream categories and the beauty of the dreamer's unique experiences.

Key Points:

• Dream experiences can be highly personal and may not always fit neatly into predefined categories.

• The diversity of dream content and meaning defies rigid classification.

• Dream interpretation is a dynamic and evolving field that embraces the complexity of dream experiences.

Highlighted Important Sections:

The Blurred Boundaries Dreams often challenge the idea of strict categorization. We explore instances where dream experiences may blur the boundaries between different dream types, creating a tapestry of unique and complex narratives.

Embracing Diversity Dream interpretation embraces the diversity of dream content and meaning. We acknowledge the vast spectrum of dream experiences and the potential for dreamers to have a wide range of personal, emotional, and transformative encounters within their dreams.

The Ever-Evolving Field Dream interpretation is a field that continues to evolve. We discuss how interpreters and scholars adapt to the changing landscape of dream experiences, embracing new insights and understanding.

As we navigate the mysteries of dream categories, we celebrate the rich tapestry of dream experiences and the evolving nature of dream interpretation.

The Exploration of Dreams in Different Cultures

Dreams hold a special place in the cultural fabric of societies around the world. In this section, we delve into the cultural significance of dreams, exploring how different cultures interpret, value, and incorporate dreams into their traditions and beliefs.

Key Points:

• Dreams have a cultural dimension, and their interpretation varies across different societies.

• The cultural context can shape the meaning and importance of dreams.

• Understanding the cultural diversity of dream interpretation enhances our appreciation of the world of dreams.

Highlighted Important Sections:

Cultural Perspectives on Dreams We explore how various cultures view and interpret dreams, highlighting differences in the role of dreams and dream symbolism in different societies.

Dreams in Indigenous Cultures often have rich traditions related to dreams and their significance. We delve into the unique practices and beliefs of these cultures concerning dreams.

Dreams in Religion Religious traditions also incorporate dreams into their beliefs. We discuss how dreams have played a role in religious experiences and prophecies in different faiths.

The Global Tapestry of Dreams By examining the cultural diversity of dream interpretation, we gain a deeper understanding of the global tapestry of dreams and how dreams connect people from all corners of the world.

As we explore the cultural dimensions of dreams, we appreciate the unique interpretations and beliefs that enrich the world of dream analysis.

Interpreting Dreams: A Personal Journey

Dream interpretation is a deeply personal journey, both for the dreamer and the interpreter. In this section, we delve into the intimate nature of dream analysis, emphasizing the importance of individual perspectives and experiences in understanding the "Meaning of Dreams."

Key Points:

• Dream interpretation is a personal and intimate process.

• The dreamer's unique experiences and emotions play a central role in understanding dream meanings.

• Interpreters guide dreamers on their journey to uncover the significance of their dreams.

Highlighted Important Sections:

The Dreamer's Perspective We explore the dreamer's role in dream interpretation, emphasizing how their individual perspective and experiences shape the meaning of their dreams.

The Intuitive Element Intuition plays a vital role in interpreting dreams. We discuss the importance of intuition in understanding the subtle nuances of dream content.

The Collaborative Process of Dream interpretation often involves collaboration between the dreamer and the interpreter. We highlight the importance of open dialogue, trust, and mutual respect in this process.

Self-Discovery and Growth The journey of dream interpretation is not solely about uncovering meanings; it is also a journey of self-discovery and personal growth. We explore how dream interpretation can lead to insights, personal development, and positive life changes.

As we explore the personal and intimate aspects of dream interpretation, we recognize the profound impact it can have on the dreamer's understanding of themselves and the world of dreams.

Dream Journals: Nurturing the Art of Dream Interpretation

Keeping a dream journal is a valuable practice for dreamers and interpreters alike. In this section, we explore the significance of dream journals in the art of dream interpretation, offering insights into how this tool can enhance the understanding of dreams.

Key Points:

• Dream journals are a tool for recording and reflecting on dream experiences.

• Keeping a dream journal helps dreamers and interpreters capture the subtleties and nuances of dreams.

• The process of journaling contributes to the growth and improvement of dream interpretation skills.

Highlighted Important Sections:

The Purpose of Dream Journals We discuss the purpose of dream journals, emphasizing their role in preserving dream memories and providing a record for interpretation.

Capturing the Details Dream journals are a means of capturing the intricate details of dreams, from imagery to emotions. We explore how this detailed record enriches the interpretation process.

Reflection and Analysis Keeping a dream journal encourages reflection on dream experiences. We discuss how the act of writing about dreams fosters insight and understanding.

Improving Interpretation Skills The consistent practice of maintaining a dream journal contributes to the growth and improvement of dream interpretation skills. We highlight the benefits of this practice for dreamers and interpreters.

Dream journals serve as a bridge between the world of dreams and the waking world, nurturing the art of dream interpretation.

Dream Symbols: The Language of the Unconscious

Dreams often communicate through symbolism, using a language that reflects the workings of the unconscious mind. In this section, we explore the role of dream symbols in dream interpretation, shedding light on how to decode the intricate language of dreams.

Key Points:

• Dream symbols are the building blocks of dream language.

• Understanding dream symbols is essential for unraveling the messages within dreams.

• Symbols may have both personal and universal meanings.

Highlighted Important Sections:

The Significance of Symbols We delve into the significance of dream symbols and their central role in dream interpretation. Understanding the language of symbols is key to uncovering the "Meaning of Dreams."

Personal and Universal Symbols Dream symbols may carry personal meanings tied to the dreamer's experiences, as well as universal associations shared by humanity. We explore the interplay between these two aspects of symbolism.

Interpreting Symbolism Deciphering dream symbols involves a nuanced process of interpretation. We discuss strategies for analyzing symbols within the context of the dream and the dreamer's unique experiences.

Conclusion: The Rich Tapestry of Dream Interpretation

In this concluding section of "Chapter 2: Types of Dreams," we reflect on the diversity and depth of dream interpretation. We emphasize the intricate nature of dreams, the personal and cultural dimensions, and the role of the interpreter in uncovering the "Meaning of Dreams."

Key Points:

• Dream interpretation is a complex and multifaceted field.

• Dreams are deeply personal, reflecting the dreamer's unique experiences and emotions.

• Cultural influences and the interpreter's insight enrich the understanding of dreams.

Highlighted Important Sections:

Celebrating Diversity We celebrate the diverse experiences of dreamers and the richness of dream content, which defies rigid categorization.

The Interpreter's Role The interpreter plays a pivotal role in guiding dreamers to explore the depths of their dream experiences. We acknowledge the importance of the interpreter's insight and intuition in the process.

The Ongoing Journey Dream interpretation is an ongoing journey, marked by self-discovery, personal growth, and a deeper understanding of the self and the world of dreams. We emphasize the dynamic and evolving nature of dream analysis.

As we conclude this chapter, we appreciate the intricate tapestry of dream interpretation and its profound impact on the understanding of the human psyche.

Chapter 3: The Role of Symbols

In "Chapter 3: The Role of Symbols," we delve into the profound significance of symbols within the realm of dreams. Symbols are the building blocks of dream language, serving as the means through which the unconscious mind communicates with the dreamer. This chapter explores the art of interpreting symbols in the context of dreams and uncovers the intricate world of dream symbolism.

Key Points:

Symbols are fundamental in dream interpretation, representing the language of the unconscious.

Understanding the multifaceted nature of symbols is essential for deciphering dream messages.

Symbols may have both personal and universal meanings, requiring a nuanced approach to interpretation.

Highlighted Important Sections:

THE LANGUAGE OF THE Unconscious

We begin by exploring the concept of dreams as a form of communication from the unconscious mind. Symbols serve as the vocabulary through which this communication takes place, conveying profound messages and insights.

PERSONAL AND UNIVERSAL Symbolism

Dream symbols may carry personal significance, tied to the dreamer's unique experiences and emotions. Simultaneously, symbols often possess universal meanings, rooted in shared human experiences and cultural associations. We delve into the dynamic interplay between these two dimensions of symbolism.

DECIPHERING SYMBOLISM

Understanding symbols in the context of dreams involves a nuanced and thoughtful approach. We discuss strategies for interpreting symbols, including analyzing their context within the dream, exploring the dreamer's experiences, and considering potential universal meanings.

THE ART OF INTERPRETATION

This section explores the interpretive skills required to unlock the depth of dream symbolism. We emphasize the role of the interpreter in guiding dreamers on their journey to decode the rich tapestry of symbols that populate the dream world.

PRACTICAL TECHNIQUES

Practical techniques for interpreting symbols are discussed, with an emphasis on fostering insight, self-discovery, and a more profound understanding of the self and the dreamer's inner world.

By the end of "Chapter 3: The Role of Symbols," readers will have gained valuable insights into the vital role that symbols play in the intricate language of dreams and the art of interpreting them.

SYMBOLISM IN EVERYDAY Life

Symbols are not confined to the world of dreams; they permeate our everyday existence. In this section, we explore the presence of symbols in our daily lives and how this interconnects with their significance in dream interpretation.

Key Points:

Symbols are prevalent in daily life, from cultural icons to personal associations.

The relationship between everyday symbols and dream symbols is examined.

Understanding the connections between the two enriches the interpretation process.

Highlighted Important Sections:

Cultural Symbols

We discuss the role of cultural symbols, such as national flags, religious icons, and historical emblems, in our daily lives. The impact of cultural symbols on our identity and values is explored.

PERSONAL SYMBOLS

Personal symbols are those that hold unique meaning for individuals based on their experiences and emotions. We delve into the significance of personal symbols and how they connect with dream symbolism.

THE INFLUENCE OF SYMBOLS

The presence of symbols in everyday life can influence dream content and interpretation. We examine how symbols from daily experiences find their way into dreams and contribute to their depth.

CROSS-CULTURAL PERSPECTIVES

This section highlights the importance of recognizing cross-cultural differences in the interpretation of symbols, as symbols may carry diverse meanings and associations in different societies.

As we explore the intersection of symbols in everyday life and dream interpretation, we gain a deeper understanding of the role symbols play in shaping our experiences and perceptions.

UNIVERSAL SYMBOLS: Shared Meanings Across Cultures

While symbols often have personal and cultural significance, there are symbols that transcend borders and cultures, carrying universal meanings and associations. In this section, we explore these universal symbols and the profound impact they have on dream interpretation.

Key Points:

Universal symbols are symbols with shared meanings across different cultures.

These symbols tap into common human experiences and emotions.

Understanding universal symbols enriches the interpretation process and broadens its cultural relevance.

Highlighted Important Sections:

EXAMPLES OF UNIVERSAL Symbols

We explore examples of universal symbols, such as the heart, the circle, and the serpent, and discuss their shared meanings and significance across diverse cultural contexts.

The Archetypal Connection

Universal symbols are often connected to archetypes, which are fundamental symbols and images present in the collective unconscious.

We delve into the archetype-symbol relationship and its role in dream interpretation.

CROSS-CULTURAL SIGNIFICANCE

The cross-cultural significance of universal symbols is examined, highlighting how these symbols resonate with people worldwide and provide a common language for dream interpretation.

INTERPRETING UNIVERSAL Symbols

Interpreting universal symbols involves understanding their shared meanings and the cultural nuances that may influence their interpretation. We discuss strategies for navigating these aspects.

By exploring universal symbols and their profound impact on dream interpretation, readers gain a more comprehensive understanding of the intricate language of dreams.

DREAM SYMBOLISM AND the Subconscious Mind

In this section, we delve into the connection between dream symbolism and the workings of the subconscious mind. We explore how symbols in dreams are intricately tied to the dreamer's inner thoughts, emotions, and experiences, offering insights into the depths of the unconscious.

Key Points:

Dream symbols are manifestations of the subconscious mind's processes.

Symbols in dreams often represent emotions, desires, fears, and unresolved conflicts.

Understanding the link between symbolism and the subconscious is crucial for meaningful dream interpretation.

Highlighted Important Sections:

SYMBOLIC REPRESENTATIONS of Emotions

We discuss how symbols in dreams often serve as representations of the dreamer's emotional landscape. Dreams provide a canvas for the subconscious to express feelings, desires, anxieties, and other inner states.

UNRESOLVED CONFLICTS and Symbolism

Symbols in dreams can mirror unresolved conflicts or issues in the dreamer's life. We explore how dream symbolism may act as a form of emotional processing and resolution.

DESIRES, FEARS, AND Dreams

Dreams are a canvas for the subconscious to project desires and fears. We examine how symbols can illuminate the dreamer's longings, aspirations, and sources of anxiety.

THE SUBCONSCIOUS AS a Dream Weaver

This section highlights the role of the subconscious mind as the creator of dream content, weaving intricate narratives through the language of symbols.

As we uncover the profound connection between dream symbolism and the subconscious mind, readers gain insights into the intricate layers of meaning embedded within dreams.

INTERPRETING SYMBOLS: A Nuanced Approach

Interpreting symbols in the context of dreams requires a nuanced and multifaceted approach. In this section, we explore the strategies and considerations that interpreters use to decipher the layers of meaning within dream symbols.

Key Points:

• Interpreting symbols is a complex process that involves considering various factors.

• Context within the dream, the dreamer's experiences, and universal meanings are all factors in interpretation.

• The role of intuition and open dialogue in the interpretation process is emphasized.

Highlighted Important Sections:

Analyzing Dream Context We delve into the importance of analyzing the context within the dream, examining how symbols interact with other dream elements and the overall narrative.

The Dreamer's Experiences The dreamer's unique life experiences and emotions play a central role in understanding the meaning of dream symbols. We discuss how these personal associations enrich interpretation.

Universal and Cultural Symbolism Interpreting symbols often involves considering both universal meanings and cultural nuances. We explore how interpreters navigate this complex interplay.

Intuition in Interpretation Intuition is a valuable tool in the interpretation process. We discuss the role of intuitive insights in unlocking the subtle nuances of symbolism.

Open Dialogue with the Dreamer Collaboration between the dreamer and the interpreter is essential in the interpretation process. We highlight the importance of open dialogue, trust, and mutual respect in fostering a deeper understanding of dream symbols.zas

By examining the multifaceted nature of symbol interpretation, readers gain a more comprehensive understanding of the art of deciphering the rich language of dreams.

Symbolism and Personal Growth

The interpretation of dream symbols extends beyond understanding the language of dreams; it also plays a significant role in personal growth and self-discovery. In this section, we explore how the process of interpreting symbols within dreams can lead to profound insights and positive life changes.

Key Points:

• The interpretation of dream symbols is a catalyst for self-discovery and personal growth.

• Symbols in dreams offer a mirror to the dreamer's inner world, encouraging introspection.

• Positive life changes and greater self-awareness can result from the exploration of symbolism.

Highlighted Important Sections:

Self-Discovery Through Symbols We discuss how the interpretation of symbols provides a pathway to self-discovery, encouraging dreamers to explore their inner world, desires, fears, and unresolved conflicts.

Positive Life Changes The insights gained through symbol interpretation can inspire dreamers to make positive life changes. We explore how this process can lead to personal growth and a more fulfilling life.

The Ongoing Journey Interpreting dream symbols is not a static process; it is an ongoing journey. We emphasize the dynamic and evolving nature of symbol interpretation as dreamers continue to explore their inner worlds.

The Role of the Interpreter. The interpreter plays a vital role in guiding dreamers on their journey of self-discovery and personal growth. We discuss the responsibilities and skills required for interpreters in this context.

As we explore the transformative power of symbol interpretation, readers gain a deeper appreciation for the profound impact it can have on the dreamer's understanding of themselves and their dreams.

Practical Techniques for Symbol Interpretation

In this section, we delve into practical techniques for interpreting symbols in dreams. These techniques are designed to assist both dreamers and interpreters in uncovering the layers of meaning hidden within dream symbols, fostering a more profound understanding of the dreamer's inner world.

Key Points:

• Practical techniques for symbol interpretation provide valuable tools for understanding dream symbolism.

• These techniques encompass methods for analyzing symbols, including free association and amplification.

• The application of these techniques enriches the interpretation process.

Highlighted Important Sections:

Free Association involves exploring the dreamer's spontaneous thoughts, feelings, and ideas related to dream symbols. We discuss how this technique uncovers hidden meanings and personal associations.

Amplification involves expanding upon the meaning of dream symbols by examining their cultural, historical, and mythological significance. We explore how amplification enriches the interpretation process.

Journaling and Reflection Keeping a dream journal and engaging in reflective practices are valuable techniques for deepening the interpretation of symbols. We discuss how these activities foster insight and self-discovery.

Visual and Creative Approaches Visual and creative techniques, such as drawing or visualizing symbols, offer unique avenues for interpreting dream symbolism. We explore how these approaches tap into the dreamer's imagination and intuition.

As we examine practical techniques for symbol interpretation, readers gain valuable tools for exploring the intricate language of dreams and uncovering the rich tapestry of symbolism.

Conclusion: The Profound Language of Dream Symbols

In this concluding section of "Chapter 3: The Role of Symbols," we reflect on the intricate and profound language of dream symbols. Symbols are the bridge between the conscious and unconscious mind, offering a unique pathway to self-discovery, personal growth, and a deeper understanding of the self.

Key Points:

• Dream symbols are the keys to unlocking the inner world of the dreamer.

• Symbol interpretation is a transformative journey that enriches the understanding of dreams and the self.

• The art of deciphering symbols in dreams holds the power to inspire positive life changes.

Highlighted Important Sections:

Celebrating Symbolism We celebrate the rich tapestry of symbolism in dreams, recognizing the diversity of symbols and their multifaceted meanings.

The Impact on Personal Growth The journey of interpreting symbols within dreams is not solely about unlocking meanings; it is also a journey of personal growth, self-discovery, and introspection.

Empowering Dreamers Dream interpretation empowers dreamers to explore their inner world, confront unresolved conflicts, and aspire to positive life changes.

The Interpreter's Role The interpreter plays a pivotal role in guiding dreamers on their journey to understand the profound language of dream symbols.

As we conclude this chapter, readers are invited to reflect on the significance of dream symbols and their transformative potential in understanding the "Meaning of Dreams."

Appendix: Symbolic Dictionary

In this appendix, we present a symbolic dictionary that serves as a valuable reference for dream interpretation. The symbolic dictionary includes a collection of common dream symbols and their potential meanings, both personal and universal.

Key Points:

• The symbolic dictionary provides a resource for understanding the meanings of various dream symbols.

• Symbols are organized alphabetically for easy reference.

• This resource assists dreamers and interpreters in uncovering the layers of symbolism within dreams.

Highlighted Important Sections:

Alphabetical Entries The symbolic dictionary features symbols organized alphabetically, making it easy to locate and explore the meanings of specific symbols.

Personal and Universal Associations For each symbol, the dictionary provides insights into potential personal associations as well as universal meanings, offering a comprehensive view of symbol interpretation.

Cross-Referencing Readers can cross-reference symbols within the dictionary to gain a broader understanding of their possible meanings and significance in dream interpretation.

The symbolic dictionary is a valuable resource for both dreamers and interpreters, aiding in the exploration of dream symbolism and the quest for deeper insights into the world of dreams.

Bibliography and Recommended Reading

In this section, we provide a bibliography and a list of recommended reading materials for those interested in delving deeper into the world of dream interpretation and symbolism. These resources offer additional insights, perspectives, and expertise to further enhance one's understanding of the subject.

Key Points:

• The bibliography includes references to academic studies, books, and articles related to dream interpretation and symbolism.

• Recommended reading materials encompass authoritative works that cover various aspects of dream analysis and symbolism.

• These resources serve as a guide for those seeking to expand their knowledge in this field.

Highlighted Important Sections:

Bibliography The bibliography contains a list of academic studies, books, and articles that have made significant contributions to the study of dream interpretation and symbolism.

Recommended Reading The section on recommended reading provides a curated list of books and texts that are highly regarded in the field of dream analysis. These materials cover a range of topics, from the psychology of dreams to the cultural and historical aspects of symbolism.

By providing access to academic sources and recommended reading materials, this section serves as a valuable reference for those who wish to continue their exploration of dream interpretation and symbolism.

Glossary of Dream Interpretation Terms

In this glossary section, we offer explanations and definitions of key terms and concepts related to dream interpretation and symbolism. This glossary serves as a helpful reference for readers to understand the terminology and concepts discussed throughout the book.

Key Points:

• The glossary provides concise definitions and explanations of important dream interpretation terms.

• It aids readers in comprehending the specialized language used in the field of dream analysis.

- The glossary enhances the reader's understanding of the subject matter.

Highlighted Important Sections:

Archetype This entry explains the concept of archetypes in dream interpretation, highlighting their role as fundamental symbols and images present in the collective unconscious.

Jungian Analysis The glossary defines Jungian analysis, outlining the approach to dream interpretation developed by Carl Jung, emphasizing the significance of the unconscious and symbolism.

Collective Unconscious This entry provides an explanation of the collective unconscious, a key concept in dream analysis, and its role in shaping the symbolism of dreams.

Projection The glossary entry for "projection" explains the psychological concept of projecting one's emotions, desires, or fears onto dream symbols.

The glossary section enhances the reader's familiarity with the specialized vocabulary and concepts central to the field of dream interpretation.

Chapter 4: Dreams and Emotions

In "Chapter 4: Dreams and Emotions," we embark on a journey to explore the intricate relationship between dreams and human emotions. Emotions are an integral part of our waking lives, and they also hold a profound connection to our dream experiences. This chapter delves into the ways in which emotions are portrayed in dreams, how they impact dream content, and the role of emotions in dream interpretation.

Key Points:

• Emotions are central to our human experience and are intricately linked to our dreams.

• Dreams often serve as a canvas for the expression of a wide range of emotions, from joy to fear, and from love to anxiety.

• Understanding the emotional dimensions of dreams enriches the interpretation process and enhances self-awareness.

Highlighted Important Sections:

Emotions in Dream Content We explore the presence of emotions in dream content, highlighting the various ways in which dreams reflect our emotional landscape.

Emotional Resonance This section delves into the emotional resonance of dreams, discussing how dreamers often wake with heightened emotions, whether positive or negative.

The Impact of Emotions on Dream Interpretation We discuss the significance of emotions in the interpretation of dreams, emphasizing how emotional analysis provides valuable insights into dream meanings.

Emotions as Dream Catalysts Dreams can be catalysts for emotional release, exploration, and self-discovery. We explore how dreamers often use dreams to process and understand their feelings.

As we journey through "Chapter 4: Dreams and Emotions," readers will gain a deeper appreciation for the intricate relationship between emotions and dream experiences and the profound impact this connection has on our understanding of the "Meaning of Dreams."

The Emotional Spectrum of Dreams

Dreams offer a canvas for the full spectrum of human emotions. In this section, we explore the diverse range of emotions expressed in dreams, from joy and love to fear and anxiety. The emotional tapestry of dreams reflects the complexity of our inner worlds.

Key Points:

• Dreams encompass a wide array of emotions, mirroring the richness of human experience.

• Positive emotions, such as happiness, love, and elation, find expression in dreams.

• Negative emotions, including fear, sadness, and anxiety, also have a place in dream content.

Highlighted Important Sections:

Joy and Elation We discuss the presence of positive emotions in dreams, emphasizing how dreams often bring feelings of joy, happiness, and elation to the dreamer.

Love and Connection Dreams frequently depict themes of love and connection, highlighting the significance of these emotions in our subconscious minds.

Fear and Anxiety Negative emotions, such as fear and anxiety, are explored in the context of dreams, shedding light on their presence and impact on dream content.

Sadness and Grief Dreams can also serve as a platform for the expression of sadness and grief, reflecting the emotional landscapes of the dreamer.

By examining the emotional spectrum of dreams, readers will gain insights into the ways in which dreams serve as a reflection of our innermost feelings and experiences.

Emotions in Dream Narratives

Emotions play a pivotal role in the narrative of dreams, influencing not only the content but also the unfolding of dream scenarios. In this section, we explore how emotions are interwoven with dream narratives, shaping the stories that dreams tell.

Key Points:

• Emotions contribute to the development and progression of dream narratives.

• Dreams often feature scenarios that evoke and reflect the dreamer's emotions.

• Understanding the emotional elements of dream narratives enhances the interpretation process.

Highlighted Important Sections:

Emotional Dream Sequences We discuss the presence of emotional dream sequences, highlighting how certain dreams are characterized by intense emotional experiences.

Narrative Resonance Emotions in dream narratives resonate with the dreamer's waking life experiences, offering a glimpse into the dreamer's inner world.

Dreams as Emotional Release This section explores the role of dreams as a means of emotional release and processing, allowing dreamers to work through their feelings.

As we delve into the connection between emotions and dream narratives, readers will gain a deeper appreciation for how emotions influence the stories that dreams tell.

The Emotional Wake: How Dreams Impact Morning Feelings

Dreams often leave an emotional residue that lingers upon awakening. In this section, we explore the emotional impact of dreams on the dreamer's morning feelings. Dreams have the power to influence our moods and emotional states upon waking, and we investigate how this phenomenon occurs.

Key Points:

• Dreams can evoke a range of emotions, leaving an emotional imprint that lasts beyond the dream itself.

• The emotional residue from dreams can affect the dreamer's mood and feelings upon waking.

• Understanding the connection between dreams and morning emotions sheds light on the emotional dimensions of dream interpretation.

Highlighted Important Sections:

Morning Feelings and Dream Content We discuss how the emotional content of dreams can influence the dreamer's mood and feelings upon awakening.

Emotional Resonance The emotional resonance of dreams extends beyond the dream state and has an impact on the dreamer's emotional well-being in the waking world.

Interpreting Morning Emotions This section explores the significance of morning emotions in dream interpretation, highlighting how they can provide valuable clues about the dream's meaning.

By examining the emotional wake left by dreams, readers will gain insights into the ways in which dreams continue to affect the dreamer long after the dream itself has ended.

Dreams as Emotional Release and Exploration

Dreams offer a unique space for emotional release and exploration. In this section, we delve into how dreams provide a canvas for dreamers to process and express their emotions, delve into their inner worlds, and gain insights into their emotional landscapes.

Key Points:

• Dreams serve as a platform for emotional release, allowing dreamers to express and process their feelings.

- Emotional exploration in dreams often leads to greater self-awareness and introspection.
- The interpretation of dream emotions offers valuable insights into the dreamer's inner world.

Highlighted Important Sections:

Catharsis Through Dreams We discuss how dreams can serve as a form of catharsis, enabling dreamers to release pent-up emotions and gain a sense of emotional relief.

Emotional Processing and Resolution Dreams often mirror unresolved conflicts or emotional dilemmas, providing an opportunity for emotional processing and resolution.

Desires, Fears, and Dreams also act as a canvas for the projection of desires and fears, allowing dreamers to explore their deepest longings and anxieties.

Self-Discovery Through Emotions Emotional exploration in dreams is a pathway to self-discovery and greater self-awareness. This section explores how dreamers can uncover hidden aspects of themselves through their emotional dream experiences.

By examining the role of dreams as a means of emotional release and exploration, readers will gain a deeper understanding of how dreams can serve as a powerful tool for processing and understanding their emotions.

Interpreting Emotional Dreams

Interpreting dreams with a strong emotional component requires a nuanced approach. In this section, we explore the strategies and considerations involved in interpreting emotional dreams, highlighting the importance of emotional analysis in uncovering the layers of meaning within these dreams.

Key Points:

- Emotional dreams are a distinct category of dreams that often carry deep emotional significance.

- Interpreting emotional dreams involves considering the emotional context, the dreamer's experiences, and the impact of emotions on dream content.
- Emotional analysis enriches the interpretation process and provides valuable insights into the dreamer's inner world.

Highlighted Important Sections:

Analyzing Emotional Context We discuss the importance of analyzing the emotional context within the dream, examining how emotions interact with other dream elements and the overall narrative.

The Dreamer's Experiences and Emotions The dreamer's unique life experiences and emotional landscape play a central role in understanding the meaning of emotional dreams. We explore how these personal associations enrich interpretation.

Emotional Impact on Dream Content Emotions have a profound impact on dream content. We delve into how emotions can shape dream scenarios and narrative development.

Symbolism and Emotion The role of symbolism in emotional dreams is examined, emphasizing how symbols often carry emotional resonance and significance.

As we explore the art of interpreting emotional dreams, readers will gain valuable insights into the nuanced approach required to understand the emotional depths of these dream experiences.

Emotional Dreams and Self-Understanding

Emotional dreams offer a unique opportunity for self-understanding and personal growth. In this section, we explore how the analysis of emotional dreams can lead to profound insights, fostering a deeper understanding of oneself and the emotions that shape one's waking and dream worlds.

Key Points:

- Emotional dreams act as a mirror to the dreamer's inner world, offering a direct reflection of their emotions and experiences.

• Analyzing emotional dreams can lead to self-discovery, enhanced self-awareness, and personal growth.

• The interpretation of emotional dreams inspires positive life changes and greater emotional well-being.

Highlighted Important Sections:

Self-Discovery Through Emotional Dreams We discuss how the interpretation of emotional dreams provides a pathway to self-discovery, encouraging dreamers to explore their inner world, desires, fears, and unresolved conflicts.

Positive Life Changes The insights gained through the analysis of emotional dreams can inspire dreamers to make positive life changes, leading to personal growth and a more fulfilling life.

The Ongoing Journey of Interpreting emotional dreams is not a static process; it is an ongoing journey of self-understanding and introspection. We emphasize the dynamic and evolving nature of this process.

The Role of the Interpreter plays a pivotal role in guiding dreamers on their journey of self-understanding and personal growth through the interpretation of emotional dreams. We discuss the responsibilities and skills required for interpreters in this context.

As we explore the transformative power of emotional dream analysis, readers will gain a deeper appreciation for the profound impact it can have on the dreamer's understanding of themselves and their emotions.

Practical Approaches to Analyzing Emotional Dreams

In this section, we delve into practical approaches and techniques for effectively analyzing emotional dreams. Emotional dreams often carry deep personal significance, and interpreting them requires specific methods to uncover their layers of meaning.

Key Points:

• Practical approaches to analyzing emotional dreams provide valuable tools for understanding their emotional content.

• Techniques for exploring emotional dreams encompass methods for emotional context analysis, symbolism, and personal associations.

• The application of these techniques enriches the interpretation process and enhances self-awareness.

Highlighted Important Sections:

Emotional Context Analysis We discuss the importance of analyzing the emotional context within emotional dreams, examining how emotions are portrayed and experienced in the dream.

Symbolic Analysis Emotional dreams often use symbolism to convey emotions. We explore how interpreters analyze the emotional significance of symbols within these dreams.

Personal Associations Understanding the dreamer's personal associations with the emotional content of the dream is essential. This section highlights how personal experiences and emotional history play a significant role in the interpretation process.

Visual and Creative Approaches Visual and creative techniques, such as drawing or journaling, offer unique avenues for exploring the emotional content of dreams. We discuss how these creative approaches tap into the dreamer's emotions and foster self-awareness.

By examining practical approaches to analyzing emotional dreams, readers will gain valuable tools for unlocking the emotional richness of these dream experiences and their profound impact on self-understanding.

Conclusion: Emotions as Dream Catalysts

In this concluding section of "Chapter 4: Dreams and Emotions," we reflect on the pivotal role that emotions play in dream experiences. Emotions serve as catalysts for the creation of dream scenarios, impacting both the content and the interpretation of dreams. As we conclude this chapter, we recognize the profound connection between emotions and dreams and their transformative potential in understanding the "Meaning of Dreams."

Key Points:

• Emotions are the driving force behind dream content, shaping narratives and scenarios.

• Emotional dreams provide a unique canvas for exploring and processing feelings.

• The interpretation of emotional dreams is a powerful tool for self-understanding, introspection, and personal growth.

Highlighted Important Sections:

The Emotive Landscape of Dreams We celebrate the diverse range of emotions portrayed in dreams, recognizing the emotional tapestry that dreams offer.

Emotions in Dream Narratives, Emotions are interwoven with dream narratives, influencing both content and storytelling.

Emotional Residue in Morning Feelings Dreams often leave an emotional imprint that affects the dreamer's morning feelings. We discuss how this emotional residue can impact one's waking life.

Emotional Dreams and Self-Understanding Interpreting emotional dreams can lead to self-understanding and personal growth. We emphasize the significance of emotional analysis in dream interpretation.

As we conclude this chapter, readers are invited to reflect on the profound role that emotions play in shaping dream experiences and their significant impact on understanding the "Meaning of Dreams."

Chapter 5: Dreams and Symbolism

In "Chapter 5: Dreams and Symbolism," we delve into the intricate world of dream symbolism. Symbols are the language of dreams, carrying rich layers of meaning that go beyond their surface appearance. This chapter explores the fundamental role of symbols in dream interpretation and how understanding the symbolism of dreams unlocks deeper insights into the subconscious mind.

Key Points:

• Dream symbolism is a central aspect of dream interpretation, where objects, actions, and scenarios hold hidden meanings.

• Symbols in dreams serve as a bridge between the conscious and unconscious mind, conveying messages and insights.

• Interpretation of dream symbolism requires a nuanced approach, considering both universal and personal associations.

Highlighted Important Sections:

Symbols: The Language of Dreams We introduce the concept of dream symbolism, emphasizing that symbols are the building blocks of the dream language. We explore how symbols convey messages from the subconscious mind.

Universal vs. Personal Symbols This section discusses the distinction between universal symbols that have common meanings across cultures and personal symbols that carry individual significance.

Analyzing Dream Symbols We delve into the methods and considerations involved in analyzing dream symbols, emphasizing the importance of context and emotional resonance.

The Art of Interpretation Dream interpretation is an art that involves unraveling the symbolism within dreams. We discuss the role of the interpreter in deciphering the meanings hidden within dream symbols.

Symbols: The Building Blocks of Dreams

In this section, we dive into the fundamental concept of dream symbolism, emphasizing that symbols are the core building blocks of the dream language. We explore how symbols convey messages from the subconscious mind and serve as the bridge between the conscious and unconscious realms.

Key Points:

• Symbols are the language of dreams, representing objects, actions, or scenarios that hold hidden meanings.

• Understanding the symbolism of dreams is essential for unlocking the messages and insights they convey.

• Symbols are the keys to unraveling the complexities of the subconscious mind and the depths of dream interpretation.

Highlighted Important Sections:

Symbolism: A Language of Metaphors We discuss how dream symbolism operates through metaphors, where everyday objects or experiences in dreams represent deeper concepts and emotions.

The Subconscious Unveiled This section delves into how symbols in dreams offer a glimpse into the subconscious mind, revealing thoughts, emotions, and experiences hidden beneath the surface.

Messages from the Unconscious Symbols in dreams are messages from the unconscious, and understanding these messages is central to dream interpretation. We explore the various types of messages conveyed through symbolism.

Context and Symbolic Interpretation The context in which symbols appear in dreams is crucial for interpretation. We discuss the role of context in unraveling the meanings behind symbols.

By examining the concept of symbols as the building blocks of dreams, readers will gain a foundational understanding of the pivotal role that symbolism plays in dream interpretation and self-discovery.

Universal vs. Personal Symbols

Dream symbols can be categorized into two main types: universal symbols and personal symbols. In this section, we explore the distinction between these types of symbols, highlighting their significance in dream interpretation.

Key Points:

• Universal symbols are symbols that carry common meanings across cultures and are widely recognized.

• Personal symbols are unique to the dreamer and have individual significance based on personal experiences and associations.

• Recognizing the type of symbol in a dream is essential for accurate interpretation.

Highlighted Important Sections:

Universal Symbols We discuss the concept of universal symbols, providing examples of symbols that have common meanings across different cultures and societies.

Personal Symbols are symbols that hold individual significance. This section explores how personal experiences and associations shape the meaning of these symbols for the dreamer.

The Intersection of Universal and Personal Symbols Dreams often contain a mix of both universal and personal symbols. We delve into how these symbols can coexist and influence each other within a dream.

The Role of Cultural and Historical Context Understanding the cultural and historical context is essential for interpreting universal symbols, as their meanings can be influenced by the society and time period in which the dreamer lives.

By exploring the differentiation between universal and personal symbols, readers will gain insights into how symbols in dreams carry distinct layers of meaning based on their nature and context.

Analyzing Dream Symbols

Interpreting dream symbols involves a nuanced analysis that considers various elements. In this section, we explore the methods and considerations involved in analyzing dream symbols, emphasizing the importance of context, emotional resonance, and the interconnectedness of symbols within dreams.

Key Points:

• Analyzing dream symbols is a multifaceted process that considers the context, emotions, and relationships between symbols.

• Context plays a pivotal role in understanding the meaning of a symbol within a specific dream.

• Emotional resonance with symbols offers valuable insights into their significance.

Highlighted Important Sections:

Context in Symbol Interpretation We discuss the significance of context in symbol interpretation, highlighting how the same symbol can have different meanings in distinct dream scenarios.

Emotional Resonance with Symbols Emotions connected to dream symbols provide clues to their meaning. We explore how emotional associations enrich the interpretation process.

Interconnected Symbols Dreams often feature interconnected symbols that form a narrative. Understanding how symbols relate to one another is essential for holistic interpretation.

The Role of the Dreamer's Experiences The dreamer's unique life experiences and associations influence the interpretation of dream symbols. We emphasize how personal experiences shape the meaning of symbols.

By examining the art of analyzing dream symbols, readers will gain insights into the depth and complexity of dream interpretation, as well as the interconnectedness of symbols within the dream language.

The Art of Interpretation

Dream interpretation is an art that involves unraveling the symbolism within dreams. In this section, we delve into the role of the interpreter in deciphering the meanings hidden within dream symbols. Interpreting dreams is a skill that requires sensitivity to context, emotions, and the unique experiences of the dreamer.

Key Points:

• Dream interpretation is a skill that involves unraveling the symbolism within dreams to reveal their meanings.

• Interpreters must consider the context, emotional resonance, and personal experiences of the dreamer in their analysis.

• Sensitivity and a nuanced approach are essential for accurate and meaningful dream interpretation.

Highlighted Important Sections:

The Interpreter's Role We discuss the pivotal role of the interpreter in guiding the dreamer through the process of understanding dream symbolism. Interpreters are facilitators of self-discovery.

Sensitivity to Context Interpreters must be sensitive to the context in which dream symbols appear, as this context often shapes the meaning of symbols.

Navigating Emotional Resonance Understanding the emotional resonance of symbols requires a deep sensitivity to the dreamer's emotions and experiences. Interpreters must navigate the emotional landscape of the dream.

Personalized Interpretation Dream interpretation is a personalized journey, and the interpretation must align with the dreamer's unique experiences and associations.

As we explore the art of interpretation, readers will gain insights into the role of the interpreter in helping dreamers unlock the meanings concealed within dream symbolism.

Conclusion: Unlocking the Language of Dreams

In this concluding section of "Chapter 5: Dreams and Symbolism," we reflect on the profound role of symbolism in dream interpretation. Symbols are the keys to unlocking the language of dreams, and understanding their meanings is central to uncovering the messages and insights concealed within the subconscious mind. As we conclude this chapter, we recognize the transformative power of symbolism in understanding the "Meaning of Dreams."

Key Points:

• Symbols are the core of the dream language, offering insights into the subconscious mind.

• Interpreting dream symbolism requires a nuanced approach that considers context, emotional resonance, and the unique experiences of the dreamer.

• Symbolism is the bridge that connects the conscious and unconscious realms of the mind.

Highlighted Important Sections:

The Language of Dreams We celebrate the richness and depth of the dream language, emphasizing how symbols are the building blocks that convey messages from the subconscious.

Universal vs. Personal Symbols The differentiation between universal and personal symbols is discussed, highlighting the significance of context and personal associations.

The Art of Interpretation Interpreting dream symbolism is an art that involves sensitivity to the unique experiences and emotions of the dreamer. We recognize the interpreter's role in guiding the dreamer on their journey of self-discovery.

Unlocking the Language of Dreams Symbolism is the key to unlocking the language of dreams, offering profound insights into the subconscious mind and fostering self-awareness and introspection.

As we conclude this chapter, readers are invited to reflect on the transformative power of symbolism in dream interpretation and the profound role it plays in understanding the "Meaning of Dreams."

Chapter 6: Dream Analysis Techniques

In "Chapter 6: Dream Analysis Techniques," we explore various methods and strategies for effectively analyzing and interpreting dreams. Dream analysis is a multi-faceted process, and this chapter delves into the practical techniques that can be employed to unravel the layers of meaning within dreams.

Key Points:

• Dream analysis techniques are essential for understanding the complex content and symbolism within dreams.

• Various methods, including Jungian analysis, Freudian analysis, and contemporary approaches, are explored.

• Each technique offers a unique perspective on dream interpretation and self-discovery.

Highlighted Important Sections:

Analyzing Dream Elements We introduce the concept of dream elements, including characters, settings, and objects, and discuss how each element contributes to the overall dream narrative.

Jungian Analysis Carl Jung's approach to dream analysis is explored, emphasizing the importance of the collective unconscious, archetypes, and symbolism in his method.

Freudian Analysis Sigmund Freud's contributions to dream analysis are discussed, including the interpretation of dreams as wish-fulfillment and the role of the unconscious mind.

Contemporary Approaches Modern and contemporary techniques in dream analysis are introduced, highlighting the evolving landscape of dream interpretation.

As we delve into various dream analysis techniques, readers will gain insight into the diverse approaches employed by dream interpreters and how these methods can be applied to gain a deeper understanding of the "Meaning of Dreams."

Analyzing Dream Elements

In dream analysis, one of the fundamental techniques involves dissecting the various elements that make up a dream. These elements encompass characters, settings, objects, and actions within the dream narrative. Understanding and interpreting each element is essential for a comprehensive analysis of the dream's meaning.

Key Points:

• Dream elements include characters (both known and unknown), settings, objects, and actions that form the dream's content.

• Analyzing dream elements provides insights into the dreamer's subconscious mind, personal experiences, and emotions.

• Interpreters carefully examine each element, considering its individual and collective significance in the dream.

Highlighted Important Sections:

Characters in Dreams We discuss the role of characters in dreams, which may include known individuals, unfamiliar figures, or even the dreamer themselves. Interpreters explore the relationships, emotions, and interactions involving these characters.

Settings and Environments Dream settings, such as locations and environments, offer important contextual information. We delve into how the choice of setting can influence the dream's meaning.

Objects and Symbols Objects within dreams often hold symbolic significance. We explore how dream analysts examine the symbolism of objects and their connections to the dreamer's emotions and experiences.

Actions and Events Dreams often feature a sequence of actions and events. These sequences are carefully dissected to uncover their underlying meanings and associations.

By examining the analysis of dream elements, readers will gain insight into the comprehensive process of unraveling the complexities of dreams and how each element contributes to the overall dream narrative.

Jungian Analysis

Carl Jung's approach to dream analysis is a significant method that emphasizes the importance of the collective unconscious, archetypes, and symbolism. In this section, we delve into Jungian analysis and how it offers a unique perspective on dream interpretation.

Key Points:

• Jungian analysis views dreams as a direct link to the collective unconscious, where universal symbols and archetypes are at play.

• Archetypes are recurrent symbols and themes that appear in dreams, representing common human experiences and emotions.

• Understanding the collective unconscious and archetypal symbolism provides insights into the deeper layers of dreams.

Highlighted Important Sections:

The Collective Unconscious We explore the concept of the collective unconscious, a universal reservoir of shared human experiences and symbols. Jungian analysis views dreams as a portal to this vast realm.

Archetypal Symbolism Archetypes are discussed as recurring symbols and themes in dreams. We provide examples of common archetypes and their significance in dream interpretation.

The Role of Symbolism Jungian analysis places great importance on dream symbolism. We discuss how symbols in dreams carry deeper meanings, often connected to archetypal themes.

Self-Discovery and Personal Growth The Jungian approach to dream analysis is closely linked to self-discovery and personal growth. We explore how understanding the collective unconscious can lead to greater self-awareness.

By examining Jungian analysis, readers will gain insights into this influential method that focuses on the deeper layers of the subconscious mind and the significance of universal symbols and archetypes in dream interpretation.

Freudian Analysis

Sigmund Freud's approach to dream analysis is a foundational method that views dreams as wish-fulfillment and explores the role of the unconscious mind in shaping dream content. In this section, we delve into Freudian analysis and its perspectives on the interpretation of dreams.

Key Points:

• Freudian analysis interprets dreams as the fulfillment of unconscious wishes and desires.

• Freud introduced concepts such as the manifest content and latent content of dreams.

• Understanding the role of the unconscious mind and repressed emotions is central to Freudian dream analysis.

Highlighted Important Sections:

Dreams as Wish-Fulfillment We discuss how Freudian analysis views dreams as a means of fulfilling unmet desires, often those suppressed in the waking state.

Manifest Content and Latent Content Freud introduced the concept of manifest content (the surface-level content of dreams) and latent content (the hidden, symbolic meaning). We explore these concepts and their importance in dream analysis.

The Unconscious Mind and Repressed Emotions Understanding the role of the unconscious mind and the emotions that are repressed in daily life is a central theme in Freudian analysis.

Sexuality and the Oedipus Complex Freudian analysis delves into the significance of sexual themes and the Oedipus complex in dream interpretation.

By examining Freudian analysis, readers will gain insights into this foundational approach to dream interpretation that emphasizes the role of repressed desires and the unconscious mind in shaping dream narratives.

Contemporary Approaches

Dream analysis is a dynamic field, and contemporary approaches offer a modern perspective on interpreting dreams. In this section, we explore various contemporary techniques and methods employed by dream interpreters to gain deeper insights into dream content and symbolism.

Key Points:

• Contemporary approaches to dream analysis reflect the evolving landscape of the field, incorporating new insights and methods.

• These approaches may incorporate elements of cognitive psychology, neuroscience, or other modern disciplines.

• Dream interpretation continues to adapt and expand with the advancement of scientific knowledge and changing cultural contexts.

Highlighted Important Sections:

Cognitive Psychology and Dream Analysis We discuss how cognitive psychology has influenced contemporary dream analysis, emphasizing the role of cognitive processes in dream narratives.

Neuroscience and Dreams The intersection of neuroscience and dream interpretation is explored, highlighting the brain's role in dream generation and perception.

The Influence of Cultural and Technological Contexts We delve into how contemporary dream analysis is shaped by cultural and technological factors, reflecting the changing landscape of human experiences.

Holistic and Integrative Approaches Some contemporary approaches adopt holistic and integrative methods that consider the physical, mental, and emotional aspects of the dreamer's life.

By examining contemporary approaches to dream analysis, readers will gain insight into the evolving nature of dream interpretation and the incorporation of modern scientific and cultural perspectives.

Holistic and Integrative Approaches

Some contemporary approaches to dream analysis adopt holistic and integrative methods that consider the physical, mental, and emotional aspects of the dreamer's life. In this section, we explore these approaches and how they aim to provide a comprehensive understanding of dreams.

Key Points:

• Holistic and integrative dream analysis takes into account multiple facets of the dreamer's life, including physical, psychological, and emotional aspects.

• The goal is to offer a well-rounded interpretation that considers the dream's context and its impact on the dreamer's well-being.

• These approaches promote self-awareness and personal growth through dream analysis.

Highlighted Important Sections:

The Mind-Body Connection We discuss the interplay between the mind and the body in holistic and integrative dream analysis. Emphasizing that physical and psychological well-being are interconnected.

Emotional Well-Being and Dream Interpretation Understanding emotions and their influence on the dreamer's overall well-being is a central theme in holistic approaches.

The Impact on Daily Life Holistic and integrative dream analysis considers how dream content may impact the dreamer's daily life, including relationships, decision-making, and personal growth.

Promoting Self-Awareness and Personal Growth The ultimate goal of these approaches is to encourage self-awareness and personal growth through the interpretation of dreams, fostering a more fulfilling and balanced life.

By examining holistic and integrative approaches to dream analysis, readers will gain insights into how these methods offer a comprehensive understanding of dreams that extends beyond symbolism and delves into the holistic well-being of the dreamer.

The Influence of Cultural and Technological Contexts

Contemporary dream analysis is shaped by the cultural and technological contexts of the times. In this section, we explore how these contexts influence dream interpretation, reflecting the changing landscape of human experiences and the tools available for dream analysis.

Key Points:

• Cultural and technological contexts influence the themes, symbols, and narratives present in dreams.

• Contemporary dream analysis incorporates the impact of cultural and technological factors on dream content and interpretation.

• Dream interpreters consider the role of culture and technology in shaping the dreamer's experiences.

Highlighted Important Sections:

Cultural Symbols in Dreams We discuss how cultural symbols, customs, and beliefs influence dream content and interpretation, emphasizing that what is significant in one culture may not be in another.

The Digital Age and Dreams The impact of technology, including the internet and social media, on dream narratives and the dreamer's experiences is explored. Contemporary dreams often feature technological elements.

Cross-Cultural Dream Analysis The globalization of culture and the exchange of ideas have led to cross-cultural dream analysis, where interpreters consider the multicultural influences on dream content.

The Shifting Landscape of Human Experiences Cultural and technological contexts continuously shape the evolving landscape of human experiences, impacting how dreams are perceived and interpreted in contemporary times.

By examining the influence of cultural and technological contexts on dream analysis, readers will gain insights into the dynamic nature of dream interpretation and how it adapts to the changing world.

Cognitive Psychology and Dream Analysis

Cognitive psychology has significantly influenced contemporary dream analysis. In this section, we explore how cognitive processes play a pivotal role in understanding dream narratives and how this approach offers fresh insights into dream interpretation.

Key Points:

• Cognitive psychology emphasizes the role of cognitive processes such as memory, perception, and problem-solving in shaping dream content.

• This approach provides a scientific perspective on the mechanisms behind dream generation and the organization of dream narratives.

• Understanding cognitive aspects of dreams enhances our comprehension of the "Meaning of Dreams."

Highlighted Important Sections:

The Role of Memory We discuss how cognitive psychology explores the role of memory in dream narratives, including the recall of past experiences and the formation of dream content.

Perception in Dreams Cognitive psychology emphasizes the role of perception in shaping dream settings, objects, and characters. It delves into how sensory experiences influence dream content.

Problem-Solving and Dream Scenarios Cognitive psychology explores the problem-solving function of dreams, where dream scenarios may serve as a means of processing daily challenges and finding solutions.

The Scientific Perspective on Dream Analysis This section discusses how cognitive psychology brings a scientific perspective to dream interpretation, focusing on empirical evidence and research in the field.

By examining the influence of cognitive psychology on dream analysis, readers will gain insights into how the study of cognitive processes enhances our understanding of the intricacies of dream content and the mind's workings.

Neuroscience and Dreams

The field of neuroscience has contributed valuable insights to the study of dreams and their interpretation. In this section, we explore the intersection of neuroscience and dream analysis, highlighting how the brain's functions play a central role in the generation and perception of dreams.

Key Points:

• Neuroscience examines the brain's role in dream generation, perception, and memory consolidation during sleep.

• This approach provides scientific explanations for dream phenomena and explores the neural processes behind dream content.

• Understanding the neuroscience of dreams enhances our knowledge of the "Meaning of Dreams."

Highlighted Important Sections:

The Brain During Dreaming We discuss how neuroscience explores the brain's activity during the dreaming process, including the activation of specific brain regions and the role of neurotransmitters.

Memory Consolidation Neuroscience delves into how dreams may contribute to memory consolidation during sleep, aiding in the retention of information and experiences.

The Scientific Study of Dreams This section emphasizes the scientific perspective of neuroscience in dream analysis, focusing on empirical research and findings in the field.

The Neural Basis of Dream Content Neuroscience offers insights into the neural basis of dream content, explaining how the brain generates dream scenarios and processes sensory information.

By examining the intersection of neuroscience and dream analysis, readers will gain a deeper understanding of the scientific aspects of dream interpretation and the brain's role in shaping dream narratives.

Conclusion: The Evolving Landscape of Dream Analysis

In this concluding section of "Chapter 6: Dream Analysis Techniques," we reflect on the diverse and dynamic approaches to dream analysis. The chapter has explored various methods, from Freudian and Jungian analysis to contemporary insights from cognitive psychology and neuroscience. As we conclude this chapter, we recognize that dream analysis is a multifaceted field that evolves with scientific advancements and cultural shifts, offering a rich tapestry of methods for understanding the "Meaning of Dreams."

Key Points:

• Dream analysis is a multifaceted field with a rich history and evolving perspectives.

• Various approaches, from psychological to scientific, provide unique insights into the interpretation of dreams.

• The chapter underscores the dynamic nature of dream analysis and its adaptability to changing times.

Highlighted Important Sections:

The Diverse Landscape of Dream Analysis We celebrate the diversity of dream analysis techniques, highlighting the multitude of perspectives that enrich the field.

Scientific Advancements and Cultural Influences The chapter emphasizes how scientific advancements and cultural contexts shape the evolving landscape of dream analysis.

A Journey of Self-Discovery Dream analysis serves as a powerful tool for self-discovery and personal growth, regardless of the method employed.

Embracing the Multifaceted Nature of Dreams, We conclude the chapter by recognizing that dreams themselves are multifaceted, and that dream analysis continues to explore their many dimensions.

As we conclude this chapter, readers are invited to appreciate the ever-evolving and diverse approaches to dream analysis and how these methods offer a comprehensive understanding of the complexities and symbolism of dreams.

Chapter 7: Interpreting Common Dream Themes

In "Chapter 7: Interpreting Common Dream Themes," we explore recurring and universal dream themes that many people experience. Dream themes often reflect common human experiences, emotions, and anxieties. This chapter delves into the interpretation of these themes, offering insights into what these dreams might signify.

Key Points:

• Common dream themes include situations like falling, flying, being chased, and more.

• These themes often have symbolic interpretations that relate to underlying emotions and experiences.

• Interpreting common dream themes can provide valuable insights into the dreamer's subconscious.

Highlighted Important Sections:

The Falling Dream We discuss the falling dream and its various interpretations, exploring how it may relate to feelings of insecurity, loss of control, or fear.

The Flying Dream Flying dreams often symbolize a sense of freedom and empowerment. We explore the emotional resonance of these dreams and their connection to personal aspirations.

Being Chased in a Dream Being chased in a dream can relate to feelings of avoidance, fear, or the need to confront something. We delve into the potential meanings of this common dream theme.

The Naked Dream The dream of being naked in public is a common theme related to vulnerability and self-image. We explore the emotional and psychological implications of this dream.

The Falling Dream

The falling dream is a recurring theme experienced by many individuals during their sleep. In this section, we explore the falling dream and its potential interpretations. Falling dreams often evoke feelings of insecurity, loss of control, or fear, and understanding the symbolism behind them can offer valuable insights into the dreamer's subconscious.

Key Points:

• Falling dreams typically involve the sensation of plummeting from a height or a feeling of unsteadiness.

• These dreams may symbolize feelings of insecurity, vulnerability, or anxiety.

• Interpretation considers the context of the dream and the dreamer's personal experiences and emotions.

Highlighted Important Sections:

The Sensation of Falling We discuss the vivid sensations associated with falling dreams, including the feeling of gravity pulling the dreamer downward.

Interpreting Fear and Insecurity Falling dreams often relate to feelings of fear and insecurity. We explore how these emotions may manifest in dream scenarios.

Context Matters The context in which the falling dream occurs is crucial for interpretation. We highlight that the circumstances and surroundings of the dream may provide additional clues.

The Unconscious Unveiled Falling dreams can offer glimpses into the dreamer's unconscious mind, revealing hidden anxieties and concerns that may not be apparent in waking life.

The Flying Dream

Flying dreams are another common and often exhilarating dream theme. In this section, we explore the flying dream and its potential interpretations. These dreams typically symbolize a sense of freedom, empowerment, and transcending limitations. Understanding the emotional resonance of flying dreams can provide valuable insights into the dreamer's aspirations and desires.

Key Points:

• Flying dreams involve the dreamer soaring through the sky or effortlessly gliding above the ground.

• These dreams are often associated with feelings of liberation, empowerment, and a desire to transcend limitations.

• Interpretation considers the emotional context and the dreamer's personal aspirations.

Highlighted Important Sections:

The Joy of Flight We discuss the exhilaration and joy often associated with flying dreams, emphasizing the freedom and empowerment they convey.

Transcending Limitations Flying dreams often symbolize the desire to overcome obstacles and limitations. We explore the emotional resonance of this theme.

Personal Aspirations Interpreting flying dreams involves understanding the dreamer's personal aspirations and how the dream reflects their desires for growth and freedom.

The Message of Empowerment These dreams often carry a message of empowerment, encouraging the dreamer to embrace their potential and seek opportunities for personal growth.

By examining the flying dream, readers will gain insights into the potential emotional and psychological meanings of this common dream theme, which often taps into the universal desire for freedom and empowerment.

Being Chased in a Dream

The dream of being chased is a frequent and anxiety-inducing theme experienced by many. In this section, we explore this common dream theme and its potential interpretations. Dreams of being chased often relate to feelings of avoidance, fear, or the need to confront something in the dreamer's life. Understanding the symbolism behind these dreams can provide valuable insights into the dreamer's subconscious.

Key Points:

• Being chased in a dream involves a pursuer or threat pursuing the dreamer.

• These dreams may symbolize feelings of avoidance, fear, or the need to confront a situation or issue.

• Interpretation considers the identity of the pursuer, the emotions evoked, and the dreamer's real-life circumstances.

Highlighted Important Sections:

The Chasing Scenario We discuss the dynamics of being chased in a dream, emphasizing the urgency and fear often associated with the pursuit.

Emotions Elicited The emotions evoked during the chase play a significant role in interpretation. We explore how the dreamer's emotional response provides valuable clues.

Identifying the Pursuer The identity of the pursuer in the dream can provide insights into what the dreamer is avoiding or confronting in their life.

Confronting Personal Challenges Being chased in a dream often relates to the need to confront personal challenges or unresolved issues. We explore the potential significance of this theme.

By examining the being chased dream, readers will gain insights into the potential emotional and psychological meanings of this common dream theme and how it reflects the dreamer's inner conflicts and fears.

THE NAKED DREAM

The dream of being naked in a public or exposed setting is a common and often embarrassing theme experienced by many individuals. In this section, we explore this common dream theme and its potential interpretations. Dreams of being naked in public often relate to feelings of vulnerability, self-image, and exposure. Understanding the emotional and psychological implications of these dreams can provide valuable insights into the dreamer's subconscious.

Key Points:

• The naked dream typically involves the dreamer being unclothed in a public or exposed situation.

• These dreams may symbolize feelings of vulnerability, self-image concerns, or fear of judgment.

• Interpretation considers the emotions evoked, the dreamer's self-image, and the context of the dream.

Highlighted Important Sections:

The Experience of Vulnerability We discuss the strong feelings of vulnerability often associated with the naked dream, highlighting how the dreamer may feel exposed and insecure.

Self-Image and Self-Esteem The dreamer's self-image and self-esteem play a central role in interpreting the naked dream. We explore how these dreams may relate to self-perception.

Fear of Judgment The fear of judgment by others is often a key theme in the naked dream. We discuss how this fear may manifest in the dreamer's experiences.

Embracing Self-Acceptance The naked dream can serve as an opportunity for self-acceptance and personal growth. We explore how these dreams can lead to greater self-awareness.

By examining the naked dream, readers will gain insights into the potential emotional and psychological meanings of this common dream theme, which often relates to issues of vulnerability, self-image, and the fear of judgment.

CONCLUSION: EXPLORING Universal Dreams

In this concluding section of "Chapter 7: Interpreting Common Dream Themes," we reflect on the significance of common dream themes and how they often relate to universal human experiences and emotions. These recurring dream themes provide a window into the dreamer's subconscious, offering insights into their fears, desires, and self-perception.

Key Points:

• Common dream themes, such as falling, flying, being chased, and being naked in public, often reflect universal human experiences and emotions.

• Interpretation of these themes considers the emotional context, the dreamer's personal experiences, and the symbolism behind the dreams.

• Dream analysis allows individuals to gain self-awareness and explore their inner world through these universal dreams.

Highlighted Important Sections:

Connecting with the Universal We celebrate the universality of common dream themes, emphasizing how people from different backgrounds and cultures may experience similar dream scenarios.

The Emotions Within Dream analysis delves into the emotional context of these dreams, revealing the dreamer's inner world and emotional concerns.

Personal Growth and Self-Exploration Through the interpretation of common dream themes, individuals have the opportunity for personal growth, self-acceptance, and self-exploration.

Unlocking the Subconscious Common dream themes often serve as a key to unlocking the subconscious, allowing dreamers to gain a deeper understanding of their inner world.

Chapter 8: Lucid Dreaming and Its Significance

In "Chapter 8: Lucid Dreaming and Its Significance," we explore the fascinating phenomenon of lucid dreaming. Lucid dreams are dreams in which the dreamer is aware that they are dreaming and can sometimes even influence or control the dream narrative. This chapter delves into the nature of lucid dreaming, its potential benefits, and how it can be a tool for self-awareness and personal growth.

Key Points:

• Lucid dreaming involves awareness within a dream, enabling the dreamer to recognize that they are in a dream state.

• The significance of lucid dreaming lies in its potential for self-awareness, creativity, and personal growth.

• We explore techniques for inducing lucid dreams and harnessing their benefits.

Highlighted Important Sections:

Understanding Lucid Dreams We discuss the fundamental nature of lucid dreams, how they differ from typical dreams, and what it means to be aware within a dream.

The Benefits of Lucid Dreaming Lucid dreaming offers various benefits, from problem-solving and creativity to confronting fears and improving sleep quality. We explore these advantages.

Techniques for Inducing Lucid Dreams Lucid dreams can be induced through specific techniques. We discuss methods that dreamers can use to increase their chances of experiencing lucid dreams.

Personal Growth and Self-Exploration Lucid dreaming can serve as a tool for personal growth and self-exploration. We delve into how dreamers can utilize this state of awareness for deeper self-understanding.

Understanding Lucid Dreams

Lucid dreams are a remarkable and intriguing aspect of dreaming in which the dreamer becomes aware that they are in a dream while the dream is still occurring. In this section, we explore the fundamental nature of lucid dreams, how they differ from typical dreams, and what it means to be aware within a dream.

Key Points:

• Lucid dreams are characterized by the dreamer's awareness that they are dreaming while the dream is unfolding.

• This awareness provides a unique and often transformative experience within the dream state.

• Lucid dreams allow the dreamer to exercise some level of control or influence over the dream narrative.

Highlighted Important Sections:

The Moment of Realization We discuss how dreamers come to the realization that they are in a lucid dream, often marked by a moment of clarity within the dream.

The Dreamer's Perspective Lucid dreams offer a distinct perspective where the dreamer is both the actor in the dream and an observer, aware of the dream's fictional nature.

Control and Influence Lucid dreaming allows the dreamer to exercise control or influence over the dream's progression, making it a unique and potentially empowering experience.

Variations in Lucidity We explore different levels of lucidity, from partial awareness to full lucidity, and how these variations impact the dreamer's experience.

The Benefits of Lucid Dreaming

Lucid dreaming offers a wide range of potential benefits and advantages beyond the realm of regular dreaming. In this section, we explore these benefits, which include problem-solving, enhanced creativity, confronting fears, and improving sleep quality. Lucid dreams can be a powerful tool for personal development.

Key Points:

• Lucid dreaming provides opportunities for creative problem-solving and generating new ideas.

• It allows dreamers to confront and overcome fears and anxieties within a safe dream environment.

• Lucid dreaming can lead to improved sleep quality and enhanced self-awareness.

Highlighted Important Sections:

Problem-Solving and Creativity We discuss how lucid dreams can be a space for brainstorming, creative inspiration, and problem-solving, offering unique solutions to real-life challenges.

Confronting Fears and Anxieties Lucid dreaming allows individuals to confront and work through fears and anxieties in a controlled dream environment, promoting personal growth and self-empowerment.

Improved Sleep Quality Lucid dreaming can lead to more restful and rejuvenating sleep, as dreamers often report feeling more in control and at ease during their dream experiences.

Self-Awareness and Personal Growth Lucid dreams can serve as a means of self-exploration and self-awareness, offering insight into one's thoughts, emotions, and desires.

Techniques for Inducing Lucid Dreams

Lucid dreams can be induced through specific techniques and practices that increase the likelihood of becoming aware within a dream. In this section, we explore some of these techniques, providing dreamers with practical methods to enhance their chances of experiencing lucid dreams.

Key Points:

• Lucid dreaming techniques often involve practices and habits that promote self-awareness during dreams.

• Techniques include reality checks, keeping a dream journal, and engaging in mindfulness.

• Consistency and patience are key to successfully inducing lucid dreams.

Highlighted Important Sections:

Reality Checks We discuss the importance of reality checks, which involve questioning the nature of one's reality and are a common practice to induce lucidity.

Keeping a Dream Journal Dream journals are valuable tools for recording and analyzing dreams. We emphasize how this practice can enhance self-awareness.

Mindfulness and Meditation Engaging in mindfulness and meditation exercises can promote self-awareness and carry over into dream awareness.

The Role of Consistency Consistency in practicing lucid dream techniques is crucial for achieving and maintaining lucid dreaming experiences.

Personal Growth and Self-Exploration through Lucid Dreaming

Lucid dreaming offers a unique opportunity for personal growth and self-exploration. In this section, we delve into how dreamers can utilize their lucid dreams to gain a deeper understanding of themselves, their thoughts, emotions, and desires. Lucid dreaming becomes a tool for self-awareness and self-improvement.

Key Points:

• Lucid dreams allow dreamers to explore their inner world, confront fears, and gain insight into their subconscious.

• The awareness within a dream provides a platform for self-empowerment, self-acceptance, and personal growth.

• Lucid dreaming can lead to profound moments of self-discovery and enhanced well-being.

Highlighted Important Sections:

Exploring the Inner World We discuss how lucid dreams offer a unique space for exploring the inner landscape of thoughts, emotions, and desires.

Confronting Fears and Challenges Lucid dreams allow individuals to confront fears and challenges in a controlled and safe dream environment, leading to personal growth and self-empowerment.

Enhanced Well-Being Lucid dreaming can contribute to improved well-being, mental health, and overall self-acceptance.

Tools for Self-Discovery We highlight how lucid dreams can serve as powerful tools for self-discovery, allowing dreamers to gain a deeper understanding of themselves and their life's journey.

Conclusion: The Profound Potential of Lucid Dreams

In this concluding section of "Chapter 8: Lucid Dreaming and Its Significance," we reflect on the profound potential of lucid dreams and their impact on personal growth, self-awareness, and overall well-being. Lucid dreams offer a unique window into the dreamer's inner world and a pathway to self-empowerment and self-discovery.

Key Points:

• Lucid dreams have the potential to unlock the dreamer's inner world, offering insights into their thoughts, emotions, and desires.

• The awareness within a dream allows individuals to confront fears, gain self-acceptance, and work toward personal growth.

• Lucid dreaming is a remarkable tool for harnessing the power of the subconscious and enhancing well-being.

Highlighted Important Sections:

A Journey of Self-Exploration We celebrate the journey of self-exploration facilitated by lucid dreaming and how it can lead to profound self-discovery.

The Transformative Power of Lucid Dreams can be transformative experiences, providing opportunities for personal growth, empowerment, and well-being.

Harnessing the Potential of the Subconscious We emphasize how lucid dreams offer a unique means of tapping into the potential of the subconscious mind.

Embracing the Profound, Lucid dreams are a gateway to the profound, allowing dreamers to explore the depths of their inner world and realize their potential for self-improvement.

Chapter 9: Dreams in Culture and History

In "Chapter 9: Dreams in Culture and History," we explore the significance of dreams in various cultures and throughout history. Dreams have played a central role in shaping cultural beliefs, spirituality, and even historical events. This chapter delves into the multifaceted relationship between dreams and human culture.

Key Points:

• Dreams have held a significant place in different cultures, influencing mythology, religion, and societal customs.

• Historical figures and events have been shaped by dreams, offering a glimpse into the power of the unconscious mind.

• We examine the cultural and historical perspectives on dreams and their role in human experience.

Highlighted Important Sections:

The Role of Dreams in Mythology We discuss how dreams have been central to the creation of myths and legends in cultures worldwide, often serving as sources of inspiration and insight.

Dreams in Religion Dreams have played a crucial role in religious experiences and revelations. We explore their significance in various faiths and spiritual traditions.

Historical Figures and Dream Accounts We highlight how historical figures, such as leaders and visionaries, have been influenced by dreams that guided their actions and decisions.

Cultural Variations in Dream Interpretation Different cultures have distinct approaches to dream interpretation. We examine how cultural contexts shape the understanding of dream symbolism.

The Role of Dreams in Mythology

Dreams have played a profound role in the creation of myths and legends in cultures around the world. In this section, we explore how dreams have often served as sources of inspiration, insight, and storytelling, influencing the formation of cultural myths and folklore.

Key Points:

• Dreams have been central to the formation of cultural myths and legends, often as vehicles for divine messages or supernatural encounters.

• Mythological narratives involving dreams convey cultural beliefs, values, and the significance of the dream state.

• We examine examples of dream-inspired myths from different cultures.

Highlighted Important Sections:

Divine Messages and Dreams We discuss how dreams are often portrayed in myths as a means through which gods or supernatural beings communicate with mortals.

The Interpretation of Dream Symbols Dreams within mythology often feature symbolic elements that hold deep cultural and spiritual meanings. We explore the interpretation of these symbols.

Dreams as Cultural Narratives Myths involving dreams provide cultural narratives that convey essential values, beliefs, and the significance of the dream experience.

Cross-Cultural Examples We present examples of dream-inspired myths and their cultural contexts, showcasing the diversity of dream-related narratives in different cultures.

Dreams in Religion

Dreams have played a crucial role in religious experiences and revelations throughout history. In this section, we explore the significance of dreams in various faiths and spiritual traditions. Dreams have been perceived as divine messages, sources of guidance, and connections to the spiritual realm.

Key Points:

• Dreams have held a central place in religious experiences and have been seen as a means of divine communication.

• Various religions and spiritual traditions have incorporated dreams into their sacred texts and practices.

• We examine the importance of dreams in different religious contexts.

Highlighted Important Sections:

Divine Revelations in Dreams We discuss how dreams have been perceived as vehicles for divine messages and revelations in numerous religious traditions.

Dreams in Sacred Texts Dreams are often mentioned in sacred texts, offering examples of dream experiences and their significance in religious contexts.

Dream Practices and Interpretation We explore how different religions and spiritual traditions have incorporated dream practices and interpretation into their rituals and beliefs.

Cultural Variations in Dream Spirituality Dreams in religion can vary across cultures and belief systems, reflecting the cultural context and interpretation of the dream experience.

Historical Figures and Dream Accounts

Throughout history, numerous historical figures, including leaders, visionaries, and influential individuals, have been influenced by their dreams. In this section, we highlight accounts of historical figures whose actions and decisions were guided by dream experiences, offering a glimpse into the power of the unconscious mind in shaping the course of history.

Key Points:

• Many historical figures have experienced significant dreams that influenced their lives, decisions, and actions.

• Dream accounts of historical figures provide insights into the role of dreams in personal and collective history.

• We explore examples of historical figures and their notable dream experiences.

Highlighted Important Sections:

Notable Historical Figures and Their Dreams We present accounts of historical figures and the dreams that had a profound impact on their lives and legacies.

Dreams Shaping History Dreams have not only influenced the lives of individuals but have also played a role in shaping historical events and movements.

The Interpretation of Dreams in History We discuss the role of dream interpretation and dream advisors in various historical periods, including ancient civilizations and royal courts.

The Unconscious in Action Dream experiences of historical figures highlight the powerful influence of the unconscious mind on human actions and decisions.

Cultural Variations in Dream Interpretation

Different cultures have distinct approaches to dream interpretation. In this section, we explore how cultural contexts shape the understanding of dream symbolism and the methods used to decipher dream messages. Dream interpretation can vary widely across cultures, reflecting diverse belief systems and traditions.

Key Points:

• Cultures around the world have unique approaches to dream interpretation, often influenced by their traditions and belief systems.

• Cultural variations in dream interpretation can involve different symbols, meanings, and practices.

• We examine examples of how dream interpretation differs across cultures.

Highlighted Important Sections:

Cultural Symbols and Meanings We discuss how specific symbols in dreams can hold different meanings in various cultures, reflecting cultural beliefs and values.

Methods of Dream Interpretation Different cultures employ distinct methods for interpreting dreams, ranging from shamanic practices to traditional symbolism.

Belief Systems and Cultural Context We explore how cultural belief systems and societal values impact the interpretation of dreams in different parts of the world.

The Universality of Dream Themes Despite cultural variations, some dream themes are universal and transcend cultural boundaries.

Conclusion: Dreams as Cultural and Historical Signposts

In this concluding section of "Chapter 9: Dreams in Culture and History," we reflect on the multifaceted relationship between dreams and culture, as well as their role in shaping historical events and personal destinies. Dreams have served as cultural and historical signposts, offering insights into the human experience and the influence of the unconscious mind.

Key Points:

• Dreams have played a significant role in the creation of cultural myths, religious experiences, and historical narratives.

• The interpretation and significance of dreams can vary widely across cultures and belief systems.

• Dream accounts of historical figures reveal the profound influence of dreams on human actions and collective history.

Highlighted Important Sections:

Cultural Significance of Dreams We celebrate the cultural significance of dreams and their role in shaping myths, narratives, and belief systems across the world.

Dreams as Historical Records Dream accounts provide valuable historical records, offering a unique perspective on the lives and actions of historical figures.

Cultural and Historical Perspectives We emphasize the diversity of cultural and historical perspectives on dreams, reflecting the rich tapestry of human experience.

The Unconscious in Human History Dreams offer a glimpse into the power of the unconscious mind and its impact on human actions, decisions, and beliefs.

Chapter 10: Dreams in the Modern World

In "Chapter 10: Dreams in the Modern World," we explore the role of dreams in contemporary society and the ways in which they are viewed and understood in the modern era. This chapter delves into the impact of technology, psychology, and cultural shifts on how dreams are perceived and analyzed in today's world.

Key Points:

• The advent of technology, including the internet and digital media, has influenced how dreams are shared and discussed.

• Modern psychology and dream research have provided new perspectives on dream analysis and interpretation.

• Dreams in the modern world continue to be a source of fascination, exploration, and personal insight.

Highlighted Important Sections:

The Influence of Technology on Dream Sharing We discuss how technology, particularly the internet and social media, has shaped the way people share and discuss their dreams with a global audience.

Dream Psychology in the Modern Era Modern psychology has advanced our understanding of dreams, leading to new approaches and interpretations in dream analysis.

Dreams in Contemporary Culture We explore the continued fascination with dreams in contemporary culture, including their presence in literature, film, and art.

Personal Growth and Self-Exploration Dreams remain a tool for personal growth and self-exploration in the modern world, offering individuals insights into their thoughts, emotions, and desires.

The Influence of Technology on Dream Sharing

Technology has profoundly impacted the way people share and discuss their dreams in the modern world. In this section, we explore how the internet, social media, and digital platforms have shaped the landscape of dream sharing, allowing individuals to connect with a global audience to share, analyze, and discuss their dream experiences.

Key Points:

• The internet and social media have provided platforms for dreamers to share their dreams with a wide online community.

• Dream sharing on digital platforms has created opportunities for collaboration, analysis, and discussion of dream experiences.

• The influence of technology on dream sharing reflects the interconnectedness of the modern world.

Highlighted Important Sections:

The Rise of Online Dream Communities We discuss the emergence of online platforms and communities dedicated to sharing and discussing dreams, fostering connections between dreamers.

Collaborative Dream Analysis Technology has enabled collaborative efforts in analyzing and interpreting dreams, with individuals worldwide contributing their perspectives.

The Global Dream Exchange We explore how the internet has made it possible for dreamers from different cultures and regions to share their dream experiences, reflecting the interconnectedness of the modern world.

Privacy and Ethics in Dream Sharing The digital realm also raises questions about privacy and ethics in sharing and analyzing dreams. We discuss these important considerations.

Dream Psychology in the Modern Era

Modern psychology has significantly advanced our understanding of dreams, leading to new perspectives and approaches in dream analysis. In this section, we explore how psychology and dream research in the modern era have contributed to the evolving interpretation of dreams.

Key Points:

• Modern psychology has provided new insights into the functions and meanings of dreams.

• Contemporary dream research focuses on the cognitive, emotional, and therapeutic aspects of dreams.

• Advances in neuroscience have deepened our understanding of the brain's activity during dream states.

Highlighted Important Sections:

The Cognitive Perspective on Dreams We discuss how modern psychology has delved into the cognitive processes involved in dreaming, including memory consolidation and problem-solving.

Dreams as Emotional Explorations Dream research now emphasizes the emotional aspects of dreams, such as how they help individuals process emotions and experiences.

Therapeutic Applications of Dream Analysis We explore how modern psychology has integrated dream analysis into therapeutic approaches, such as dream interpretation and dream journaling.

The Role of Neuroscience Advances in neuroscience have shed light on the brain's activity during dreams, contributing to our understanding of the physiological aspects of dreaming.

Dreams in Contemporary Culture

Dreams continue to hold a significant place in contemporary culture, with their presence felt in literature, film, art, and various creative expressions. In this section, we explore how dreams are depicted and interpreted in modern culture and how they continue to captivate the imagination of artists, writers, and thinkers.

Key Points:

- Dreams remain a source of inspiration and fascination for contemporary artists and creators.
- They are often depicted in literature, film, and art as sources of symbolism, creativity, and exploration.
- The interpretation of dreams in modern culture reflects the ongoing intrigue with the dream state.

Highlighted Important Sections:

Dreams in Literature and Poetry We discuss how dreams are woven into contemporary literature and poetry, serving as rich sources of symbolism and creativity.

Dreams on the Silver Screen The world of cinema continues to explore and depict dreams as elements of storytelling and imagination. We highlight notable examples in film.

Dreams in Visual Art Dreams have inspired artists to create thought-provoking works of art. We explore the role of dreams in visual culture.

The Interpretation of Dreams in Pop Culture The interpretation of dreams in contemporary culture reflects the ongoing fascination with the dream state and its potential for self-discovery and creativity.

Personal Growth and Self-Exploration

Dreams continue to serve as a tool for personal growth and self-exploration in the modern world. In this section, we delve into how individuals use their dream experiences to gain insights into their thoughts, emotions, and desires. The dream state remains a valuable platform for self-awareness and personal development.

Key Points:

- Modern individuals utilize their dream experiences as a means to explore their inner world, confront fears, and gain insight into their subconscious.
- The dream state is considered a platform for personal growth, self-acceptance, and enhanced well-being.

• Dreams remain a source of fascination and exploration for those seeking self-awareness and personal development.

Highlighted Important Sections:

Dream Journaling for Self-Reflection We discuss the practice of keeping a dream journal as a valuable tool for self-reflection and exploring the inner landscape of the mind.

Confronting Fears and Challenges Dreams provide a controlled environment for individuals to confront fears and challenges, leading to personal growth and self-empowerment.

Enhanced Well-Being and Mental Health Dreams can contribute to improved well-being and mental health, providing opportunities for self-acceptance and inner exploration.

Tools for Self-Discovery The dream state continues to offer individuals unique tools for self-discovery, allowing them to gain deeper understanding of themselves and their life journey.

Conclusion: The Perpetual Significance of Dreams

In this concluding section of "Chapter 10: Dreams in the Modern World," we reflect on the enduring significance of dreams in contemporary society. Despite the changes brought about by technology, psychology, and culture, dreams remain a powerful source of fascination, exploration, and self-discovery in the modern era.

Key Points:

• Dreams continue to hold a central place in contemporary culture, providing inspiration, creativity, and exploration.

• Modern psychology has deepened our understanding of the dream state, contributing to new perspectives on dream analysis.

• The interpretation of dreams in the modern world reflects the ongoing intrigue with the dream state and its potential for personal growth and self-awareness.

Highlighted Important Sections:

The Timelessness of Dream Exploration We celebrate the timeless appeal of dream exploration, which transcends technological and cultural changes.

The Multifaceted Nature of Dreams continue to be multifaceted, offering sources of symbolism, creativity, and personal insight in the modern world.

The Unfinished Story of Dreams The story of dreams is ongoing, with new chapters written as technology, psychology, and culture continue to shape our understanding of the dream state.

The Enduring Appeal of Dreams persist as a source of fascination and exploration, offering individuals the opportunity to delve into their inner worlds.

Chapter 11: The Future of Dream Exploration

In "Chapter 11: The Future of Dream Exploration," we explore the possibilities and potential advancements in the field of dream analysis. This chapter delves into emerging technologies, evolving psychological insights, and the ways in which dreams may continue to be explored and understood in the years to come.

Key Points:

• Emerging technologies, such as neuroimaging and artificial intelligence, may offer new avenues for understanding dreams.

• Evolving psychological research is likely to contribute to a deeper understanding of the functions and meanings of dreams.

• The future of dream exploration is a fascinating frontier that holds promise for further insights into the human mind.

Highlighted Important Sections:

Advancements in Dream Analysis We discuss emerging technologies and their potential to enhance our understanding of dreams, including neuroimaging and AI.

Psychological Insights on the Horizon The evolving field of psychology may offer new perspectives on the functions and meanings of dreams, contributing to a richer understanding.

The Intersection of Science and Dreaming We explore the exciting possibilities at the intersection of scientific research and dream analysis, including studies on the brain's activity during dreams.

The Ongoing Quest for Understanding The future of dream exploration holds promise for further insights into the human mind, offering a fascinating frontier for research and discovery.

Advancements in Dream Analysis

Emerging technologies and scientific advancements have the potential to revolutionize the field of dream analysis. In this section, we explore how technologies such as neuroimaging and artificial intelligence (AI) may offer new avenues for understanding the intricate world of dreams.

Key Points:

• Emerging technologies like neuroimaging provide insights into the brain's activity during dream states.

• Artificial intelligence can help analyze and interpret dream content more efficiently.

• Advancements in dream analysis hold the promise of unraveling the complex functions and meanings of dreams.

Highlighted Important Sections:

Neuroimaging and Dream States We discuss how neuroimaging techniques, such as functional magnetic resonance imaging (fMRI), are used to study brain activity during dreams, shedding light on the neural correlates of dream experiences.

AI in Dream Interpretation Artificial intelligence and machine learning are increasingly applied to analyze and interpret dream content, potentially providing more accurate and efficient insights.

Interdisciplinary Approaches The combination of neuroscience, psychology, and technology allows for interdisciplinary approaches to dream analysis, offering a holistic understanding of dreams.

The Promise of Future Discoveries Advancements in dream analysis open the door to future discoveries that may deepen our understanding of the subconscious mind.

The Intersection of Science and Dreaming

The intersection of scientific research and dream analysis holds the potential for groundbreaking insights into the nature and functions of dreams. In this section, we explore the exciting possibilities at the nexus of scientific inquiry and the exploration of dream states.

Key Points:

• Scientific research is uncovering the neurological and physiological underpinnings of dreams.

• Studies on the brain's activity during dream states are providing valuable information about the nature of dreaming.

• The intersection of science and dream analysis offers a unique perspective on the dream state.

Highlighted Important Sections:

Neurological Studies on Dreaming We discuss how scientific studies have contributed to our understanding of the neurological processes involved in dreaming.

Physiological Aspects of Dreams Physiological measurements, such as REM (Rapid Eye Movement) sleep studies, offer insights into the physiological aspects of dream states.

The Brain's Activity During Dreams Research on the brain's activity during dreams, often through neuroimaging techniques, is revealing the neural correlates of dream experiences.

The Promise of Interdisciplinary Research, which combines neuroscience, psychology, and other fields, provides a holistic approach to studying dreams.

Psychological Insights on the Horizon

The field of psychology continues to evolve, and this evolution holds the promise of contributing to a deeper understanding of the functions and meanings of dreams. In this section, we explore how evolving psychological research may shape the future of dream analysis.

Key Points:

• Ongoing psychological research is likely to uncover new insights into the psychological aspects of dreams.

• Developments in cognitive psychology, emotional psychology, and consciousness studies can shed light on dream phenomena.

• Psychological insights may offer a more comprehensive understanding of the roles dreams play in our lives.

Highlighted Important Sections:

Cognitive Psychology and Dream Functions We discuss how cognitive psychology is being used to explore the functions of dreams, including memory consolidation and problem-solving.

Emotional Psychology and Dream Analysis The emotional aspects of dreams are a focus of study in the evolving field of emotional psychology, offering insights into how dreams help individuals process emotions.

Consciousness Studies and Dream States are a topic of interest in the study of consciousness, as researchers delve into altered states of awareness during dreams.

The Quest for Comprehensive Understanding Psychological insights offer a pathway to comprehensively understand the complex roles dreams play in human psychology and experience.

The Intersection of Science and Dreaming

The intersection of scientific research and dream analysis holds the potential for groundbreaking insights into the nature and functions of dreams. In this section, we explore the exciting possibilities at the nexus of scientific inquiry and the exploration of dream states.

Key Points:

• Scientific research is uncovering the neurological and physiological underpinnings of dreams.

• Studies on the brain's activity during dream states are providing valuable information about the nature of dreaming.

• The intersection of science and dream analysis offers a unique perspective on the dream state.

Highlighted Important Sections:

Neurological Studies on Dreaming We discuss how scientific studies have contributed to our understanding of the neurological processes involved in dreaming.

Physiological Aspects of Dreams Physiological measurements, such as REM (Rapid Eye Movement) sleep studies, offer insights into the physiological aspects of dream states.

The Brain's Activity During Dreams Research on the brain's activity during dreams, often through neuroimaging techniques, is revealing the neural correlates of dream experiences.

The Promise of Interdisciplinary Research, which combines neuroscience, psychology, and other fields, provides a holistic approach to studying dreams.

The Ongoing Quest for Understanding

The future of dream exploration holds promise for further insights into the human mind and the intricate world of dreams. In this section, we discuss the evolving landscape of dream analysis and the continuous quest to unravel the complex functions and meanings of dreams.

Key Points:

• Advancements in technology, psychology, and interdisciplinary research offer exciting possibilities for understanding dreams.

• The evolving field of dream analysis is marked by ongoing discoveries and the pursuit of comprehensive insights into the dream state.

• The dream state remains a fascinating frontier for those seeking to explore the depths of human consciousness.

Highlighted Important Sections:

Uncharted Territories in Dream Exploration, We delve into the uncharted territories of dream exploration and the potential for future discoveries.

The Role of Dream Researchers and Enthusiasts Dream researchers and enthusiasts continue to push the boundaries of dream analysis, contributing to the ever-growing body of knowledge.

The Endless Potential of Dream Analysis The study of dreams remains open to endless possibilities, offering a rich field of exploration for those seeking to understand the human mind.

Dreams and Human Consciousness Dreams provide a unique window into the depths of human consciousness, offering valuable insights and revelations.

Conclusion: The Dreaming Horizon

In this concluding section of "Chapter 11: The Future of Dream Exploration," we reflect on the boundless potential and ongoing quest for understanding the intricate world of dreams. The future of dream exploration is a horizon filled with exciting possibilities, offering the opportunity to delve deeper into the human mind and consciousness.

Key Points:

• The future of dream exploration holds limitless potential for uncovering the secrets of the dream state.

• Advancements in technology, psychology, and interdisciplinary research offer a path to more comprehensive insights into dreams.

• The dream state continues to inspire, captivate, and challenge those who seek to understand its profound mysteries.

Highlighted Important Sections:

A World of Endless Discovery We celebrate the world of endless discovery that the future of dream exploration offers, as researchers and dream enthusiasts continue to push the boundaries of knowledge.

The Quest for Comprehensive Understanding The pursuit of comprehensive understanding is at the heart of the future of dream analysis, where science and the human spirit converge.

The Ever-Present Fascination with Dreams Despite the progress in technology and psychology, the fascination with dreams remains a constant, inspiring those who seek to explore their depths.

A Dreaming Horizon The future of dream exploration is a horizon of boundless potential, offering the opportunity to unlock the secrets of the dream state.

As we conclude this chapter and the book, readers are invited to contemplate the limitless possibilities and ongoing quest for understanding the world of dreams. The future of dream exploration is a horizon filled with promise, where science and human curiosity continue to intersect.

Common Dreams and Their Interpretations

Introduction: The Universality of Common Dreams
• A brief introduction to the concept of common dreams and how they transcend cultural boundaries.

• Mention that while individual dream experiences are unique, some dreams are widely reported and have recurring themes.

1. Falling Dreams

• Falling dreams are among the most prevalent, often involving the sensation of plummeting from a height. These dreams may be accompanied by a racing heart and a sudden jolt awake.

• Interpretation: Falling dreams can signify a lack of control or stability in one's life. The feeling of falling represents a fear of losing ground or failing in some aspect of life, whether it's personal or professional.

2. Flying Dreams

• Flying dreams evoke a sense of freedom and euphoria as one soars effortlessly through the sky. The dreamer often experiences exhilaration and joy during these dreams.

• Interpretation: Flying dreams are commonly associated with the desire for liberation, the need to break free from limitations, or the yearning to transcend everyday boundaries. They reflect a deep longing for independence and the courage to rise above life's challenges.

3. Being Chased Dreams

• Dreams of being chased create a sense of panic and anxiety, as the dreamer is relentlessly pursued by an unknown or threatening force. Running or hiding are common responses in these dreams.

• Interpretation: These dreams often symbolize unresolved issues, fears, or stressors in the dreamer's life. The pursuer can represent problems or emotions that one is trying to avoid but need to confront.

4. Teeth Falling Out Dreams

• Dreams in which teeth fall out can be unsettling, as the dreamer may experience a loss of teeth with varying emotions, from embarrassment to fear.

• Interpretation: These dreams are frequently linked to concerns about appearance, communication, or a perceived loss of power or control. They may reflect feelings of vulnerability related to self-image and self-expression.

5. Naked in Public Dreams

• Dreams of being naked in public can induce feelings of vulnerability, embarrassment, and exposure as the dreamer is suddenly revealed without clothing in a crowd.

• Interpretation: Such dreams often point to concerns about self-esteem, fear of judgment, or the desire to hide one's true self from others. They may highlight a need for acceptance and self-confidence.

6. Test or Exam Dreams

• Test or exam dreams commonly occur in academic or professional settings, where the dreamer feels unprepared and under pressure to perform well.

• Interpretation: These dreams can indicate anxieties related to competence, preparation, or the evaluation of one's abilities. They may reflect the fear of falling short of expectations or failing to meet important goals.

7. Falling Behind Dreams

• Dreams of falling behind or being late are characterized by the distressing sense of not keeping up with deadlines, schedules, or responsibilities.

• Interpretation: Such dreams often signify concerns about being overwhelmed, missing opportunities, or not meeting expectations in various areas of life. They can reflect the dreamer's fear of not being able to catch up or maintain control.

Conclusion: The Richness of Dream Interpretation

• Summarize the section's key points about common dreams and their interpretations.

• Emphasize that while these dreams are frequent, individual experiences may vary, and interpretation is a deeply personal and subjective process.

Conclusion: The Dreamer's Odyssey

As we reach the final pages of this journey through the enigmatic world of dreams, we stand at the threshold of profound insight and endless wonder. Our exploration has traversed the ages, from the mystical interpretations of ancient cultures to the cutting-edge insights of modern science. It has been a voyage through the depths of human consciousness, where dreams, like constellations in the night sky, continue to guide us, inspire us, and awaken our innermost desires.

In "Dictionary of Dream Interpretation," we've unraveled the meanings and symbolism woven into the tapestry of the dream state. We've explored the cognitive, emotional, and therapeutic facets of dreams, discovering their role in our personal growth, creative expression, and self-exploration. We've witnessed the ever-continuing fascination with dreams, as they inspire artists, writers, and thinkers to delve into the recesses of the human psyche.

Our journey has extended beyond the limits of the past, with a glimpse into the horizon of the future. Emerging technologies, evolving psychological insights, and the unceasing spirit of exploration promise a new era of understanding the intricate world of dreams.

In your hands, this book becomes not only a guide but a passport to the boundless landscapes of your own mind. As you close these pages, we invite you to reflect on the infinite possibilities that dream exploration offers. The stories, emotions, and insights they bring are yours to discover and interpret, just as countless dreamers have done throughout history.

We extend our deepest gratitude to you, dear reader, for accompanying us on this odyssey through the dreamer's world. Your curiosity, your quest for understanding, and your willingness to explore the depths of your own dreams are the very essence of this book's journey.

In the words of the great dreamer Carl Jung, "Who looks outside, dreams; who looks inside, awakes." We hope this book has encouraged you to awaken, to look within, and to embark on your own voyage through the enigmatic landscape of your dreams.

Thank you for sharing this adventure with us, and may your dreams continue to guide and inspire you on your own unique odyssey.

With heartfelt thanks and warm wishes,

Daniel Sanjurjo

Did you love *The Dreams Interpretation Book*? Then you should read *Astrology Unveiled: Your Guide to the Zodiac*[1] by The fun book creators!

UNLOCK THE MYSTERIES of the Cosmos with "Celestial Wisdom: An Astrologer's Journey"

⟡ Are you ready to embark on a profound astrological journey that will illuminate your path to self-discovery, personal growth, and decision-making? "Celestial Wisdom: An Astrologer's Journey" is your definitive guide to the enchanting world of astrology.

⟡ Explore the Foundations of Astrology: Delve into the origins of astrology, the celestial bodies that influence our lives, and the intricate language of the zodiac. From the sun signs to birth charts, this book unravels the enigma of the stars.

◇ Debunking Myths and Discovering Realities: Address common misconceptions and criticisms surrounding astrology while gaining a deeper understanding of the scientific perspective on this ancient practice. Let the stars guide you on your path to wisdom.

◇ In-Depth Zodiac Sign Insights: Embark on a journey through the twelve zodiac signs, each filled with tailored insights, predictions, and guidance for every aspect of life. The zodiac's influence on your personality, career, love life, and more will be unveiled.

◇ Resources for Further Study: If you're eager to explore astrology beyond the pages of this book, our comprehensive resource section offers a guide to books, websites, and courses that will enrich your astrological knowledge.

◇ Conclusion and Beyond: Conclude this mesmerizing voyage through the cosmos with a heartfelt reflection on the enduring wisdom of astrology. Unearth the stories the stars have written for you.

◇ We encourage you to continue your exploration of the celestial realms, seeking the wisdom of the cosmos to guide your unique path.

Your journey has only just begun.

This illustrated guide invites you to embrace the wisdom of the stars and unlock the tapestry of your life. Are you ready to embrace "Celestial Wisdom"? The universe awaits your discovery.

Also by Daniel Sanjurjo

The Dreams Interpretation Book

About the Author

DANIËL SANJURJO IS a passionate author who delves into the realms of astrology and self-help. With a gift for exploring the celestial and the human psyche, Daniël's books are celestial journeys of self-discovery and personal growth. Join the cosmic odyssey with this insightful writer.

Don't miss out!

Visit the website below and you can sign up to receive emails whenever Daniel Sanjurjo publishes a new book. There's no charge and no obligation.

https://books2read.com/r/B-A-WQHBB-DKEQC

BOOKS 2 READ

Connecting independent readers to independent writers.

Did you love *Dreams Interpretation Guide*? Then you should read *Cosmic Revelations 2024*[1] by Daniel Sanjurjo!

[2]

Cosmic Revelations: Embracing the Wonders of the Universe. Are you ready to discover the wonders of the universe and embrace cosmic revelations? "Cosmic Revelations" is the ultimate guide that takes you on a profound journey through the cosmos, revealing the secrets of the universe.

Explore the mysteries of the universe, from the birth of stars and galaxies to the secrets of dark matter. Discover fascinating insights about the solar system, black holes, and the evolution of life in the universe.

Uncover the secrets of the universe and embrace cosmic revelations that will transform your understanding of the world. Expand your

---

1. https://books2read.com/u/bwBeZe

2. https://books2read.com/u/bwBeZe

knowledge of astronomy and astrophysics, and gain a deeper appreciation of the wonders of the universe.

Dive into "Cosmic Revelations" and embark on an unforgettable journey of discovery. Learn about the latest scientific discoveries and breakthroughs in astrophysics. Gain a better understanding of the universe and your place in it.

Conclude this mesmerizing voyage through the cosmos with a new perspective on the wonders of the universe. Embrace cosmic revelations and unlock the limitless potential of your universe. Start your journey today with "Cosmic Revelations" and discover a whole new world of possibilities.

Also by Daniel Sanjurjo

Zodiaco

Piscis 2024: Un Viaje Celestial

Zodiac world

Aries Revealed 2024

Taurus 2024

Leo 2024

Gemini 2024

Cancer horoscope 2024

Virgo 2024

Scorpio 2024

Sagittarius 2024 Horoscope

Capricorn 2024

Aquarius 2024

Standalone

Cosmic Revelations 2024

Dreams Interpretation Guide